WHERE DO

WE GO FROM

HERE?

WHERE DO WE GO FROM HERE?

HOW TOMORROW'S PROPHECIES FORESHADOW TODAY'S PROBLEMS

STUDY GUIDE | TEN LESSONS

DR. DAVID JEREMIAH

HarperChristian
Resources

Where Do We Go From Here? Study Guide
© 2021 by Dr. David P. Jeremiah
P.O. Box 3838, San Diego, CA 92163

Requests for information should be addressed to:
HarperChristian Resources, 3900 Sparks Dr. SE, Grand Rapids, Michigan 49546

ISBN 978-0-310-14095-5 (softcover)
ISBN 978-0-310-14094-8 (ebook)

Published in association with Yates & Yates, www.yates2.com.

Contents

How to Use This Study Guide

The purpose of this study guide is to reinforce Dr. David Jeremiah's dynamic, in-depth teaching and to aid you in applying biblical truth to your daily life. This study guide is designed to be used in conjunction with *Where Do We Go From Here?* by Dr. David Jeremiah, but it may also be used by itself for personal or group study.

Structure of the Lessons

Each lesson is based on the corresponding chapter in *Where Do We Go From Here?* and focuses on specific passages in the Bible. Each lesson is composed of the following elements:

- **Outline:** The outline at the beginning of the lesson gives a clear, concise picture of the topic being studied and will provide a helpful framework for you as you go through Dr. Jeremiah's teaching or read the book.

- **Overview:** The overview summarizes Dr. Jeremiah's teaching on the passage being studied in the lesson. You should refer to the Scripture passages in your own Bible as you study the overview. Unless otherwise indicated, Scripture verses quoted are taken from the New King James Version.

- **Application:** This section contains a variety of individual and group discussion questions designed to help you dig deeper into the lesson and the Scriptures and to apply the lesson to your daily life. For Bible study groups or Sunday school classes, these questions will provide a springboard for group discussion and interaction.

- **Did You Know?** This section presents a fascinating fact, historical note, or insight that adds a point of interest to the preceding lesson.

Personal Study

The lessons in this study guide were created to help you gain fresh insights into God's Word and develop new perspectives on topics you may have previously studied. Each lesson is designed to challenge your thinking and help you grow in your knowledge of Christ. During your study, it is our prayer that you will discover how biblical truth affects every aspect of your life and your relationship with Christ will be strengthened.

When you commit to completing this study guide, try to set apart a time, daily or weekly, to read through the lessons without distraction. Have your Bible nearby when you read the study guide so that you're ready to look up verses if you need to. If you want to use a notebook to write down your thoughts, be sure to have that handy as well. Take your time to think through and answer the questions. If you plan on reading the study guide with a small group, be sure to read ahead and be prepared to take part in the weekly discussions.

Group Study

The lessons in this study guide are suitable for Sunday school classes, small-group studies, elective Bible studies, or home Bible study groups. Each person in the group should have his or her own study guide. You may wish to complete the study guide lesson as homework prior to the meeting of the group and then use the meeting time to discuss the lesson. If you are a group leader, refer to the guide at the back of this book for additional instructions on how to set up and lead your group time.

For Continuing Study

For a complete listing of Dr. Jeremiah's materials for personal and group study, call 1-800-947-1993, go online to www.DavidJeremiah.org, or write to Turning Point, P.O. Box 3838, San Diego, CA 92163.

Dr. Jeremiah's *Turning Point* program is currently heard or viewed around the world on radio, television, and the Internet in English. *Momento Decisivo*, the Spanish translation of Dr. Jeremiah's messages, can be heard on radio in every Spanish speaking country in the world. The television broadcast is also broadcast by satellite throughout the Middle East with Arabic subtitles.

Contact Turning Point for radio and television program times and stations in your area, or visit our website at www.DavidJeremiah.org/stationlocator.

Where Do We Go From Here?

Perhaps you remember the collapse of the Champlain Towers South condominium building in Surfside, Florida. In the dead of night, one floor pancaked onto the next, burying scores of people under tons of concrete. Most were sleeping in their beds, unaware of the suddenness of the coming catastrophe. There had been signs—warnings of water seeping beneath critical parts of the structure and weakening its integrity. But the alarm sounded too late.

In a similar way, the underpinnings of our culture are weakening. The eroding foundations and structural cracks of our nation and world are nearing collapse. We must sound the alarm. We need to know the times and anticipate the return of Christ. We see the signs of the times in the events now unfolding.

These events, which we'll cover in this study, are not isolated movements, philosophies, or circumstances. They are as interconnected as a spider's web. A future pandemic could lead to emerging globalism. Meanwhile, our worldwide economy hangs by a strand. The world is filled with people who are lovers of pleasure more than lovers of God—and ready to cancel anyone who disagrees with them. This translates to extreme persecution for the Church in much of the world and to eroding religious liberty at home. An unprecedented spiritual famine is causing an epidemic of emaciated hearts. Many professed Christians are abandoning the faith, creating a vacuum for the rising tide of Marxism. Simultaneously, events in the Middle East are turning Jerusalem into the powder keg of history.

But this is no time to be discouraged! The Gospel will triumph as surely as Christ rose from the dead. Jesus is Lord, and history belongs to Him. We're privileged to be His agents in these perilous times. And it's time to live by conviction. When Moses sent the spies into the Promised Land to reconnoiter the territory, ten of them were overwhelmed with fear. But two of the spies, Joshua and Caleb, were ready to go forward and take the land! Caleb later told Joshua, "I brought him back a report according to my convictions" (Joshua 14:7, NIV).

We cannot live by lies. We must live by our biblical convictions. We can no longer ignore the warnings or sleep in beds of ignorance. We're approaching the consummation of the ages.

In this study, we'll deal with ten prophetic issues as current as the morning news. We'll thread our way through problems that Jesus predicted—precursors of the Tribulation, and we'll learn how we should do the next best thing. Even as the world collapses, the Lord is building His Church. We can say something, do something, pray something, preach something, and live by the convictions of Christ.

God's people are more than conquerors. We have a way forward. At any moment, Jesus Christ will descend from heaven for His people. We haven't long to wait. But until then, we need to understand what the age requires and to do as the Lord commands.

Ezekiel 22:30 says: "I searched for a man among them who would repair the wall and stand in the gap before me on behalf of the land so that I might not destroy it, but I found no one" (CSB).

May the Lord find us, and may He find us faithful in these days. Don't be fearful, and don't let the times overwhelm you. This world will not end in rubble, but in His return! Our risen and exalted Lord Jesus Christ, our enthroned Savior—He knows the way forward.

He will show us where to go from here.

LESSON 1

A CULTURAL PROPHECY— SOCIALISM

MATTHEW 24:37

In this lesson we learn about the dangers of socialism and how it differs from how Christ wants His followers to live.

Venezuela was once the wealthiest nation in South America, with a per capita income almost rivaling that of the United States. The people enjoyed religious liberty, political freedom, personal dignity, and economic opportunity. Today, record numbers of Venezuelan migrants are fleeing northward, and Venezuela is tumbling into anarchy. What caused this dramatic descent into chaos? Marxist president Hugo Chávez relentlessly implemented the socialist playbook, followed by his equally socialist and dictatorial Marxist successor, Nicolás Maduro. The lessons for us are stark.

OUTLINE

I. What Does This Mean?
    A. The Destruction of Monuments
    B. Cancel Culture
    C. The Dismantling of the Nuclear Family
    D. The Redistribution of Wealth
    E. Defunding the Police

II. **Where Do We Go From Here?**
  A. Review What the Bible Says
  B. Refuse to Live by Lies
  C. Resolve to Follow Christ and Not Just Admire Him
  D. Rethink Small Groups
  E. Resist Any Way You Can
  F. Remember Venezuela

OVERVIEW

Today's socialist agendas are distressing to anyone who has studied social-ism and communism. Second Timothy 3:1 says, "But understand this, that in the last days dangerous times [of great stress and trouble] will come, [difficult days that will be hard to bear]" (AMP). Jesus said it like this: "But as the days of Noah were, so also will the coming of the Son of Man be" (Matthew 24:37).

Genesis 6:5 describes the days of Noah: "Every intent of the thoughts of [man's] heart was only evil continually." We aren't far off from the wick-edness of Noah's day. Socialism creates great stress and trouble, difficult days that are hard to bear. It demands a one-world system of government, reminiscent of biblical prophecy.

Revelation 13 describes the Antichrist: "He was given authority to rule over every tribe and people and language and nation." (Revelation 13:7, NLT). Satan "deceives the whole world" (Revelation 12:9), and the False Prophet will "deceive those who dwell on the earth" (Revelation 13:14). The Lord warns us: "Beware lest anyone cheat you through philosophy and empty deceit, according to the tradition of men, according to the basic prin-ciples of the world, and not according to Christ" (Colossians 2:8).

Marxism cheats people through philosophy and empty deceit. Karl Marx's systems have led to horrific scenes. His own family and friends con-sidered him to be possessed by a demon, and in a poem he said, "My soul, once true to God, is chosen for hell."

Marxism is anti-God. Karl Marx hated Christianity. To him, religion was "the opium of the people." For communism to succeed, loyalty to the

Church had to be replaced by loyalty to the state. On one occasion, he described the Church as "This medieval mildew which must be scraped away." Each successive leader saw organized religion as an enemy—a competitor that needed to be controlled or eliminated.

Marxism is totalitarian. Marxism quickly becomes totalitarian. Fascist dictator Benito Mussolini summed it up this way: "Everything within the state, nothing outside the state, nothing against the state."

Rod Dreher adds: "Today's totalitarianism demands allegiance to a set of progressive beliefs, many of which are incompatible with logic—and certainly with Christianity. Compliance is forced less by the state than by elites who form public opinion, and by private corporations that, thanks to technology, control our lives far more than we would like to admit."[1]

Marxism is divisive. Marxism thrives on division. In historic Marxism the division was promoted between classes of people. In today's cultural Marxism, the exploited divide is often racial, sexual, or gender related. Whenever a socialist or Marxist can't figure out how to respond to an issue, they call it racist.

This is tragic for many reasons. It's very hurtful to be branded a racist when one has done or said nothing that would lead a rational person to make such an accusation. Once racism has been pinned on a person, it's almost impossible to get rid of the label. But there's another seldom-discussed sadness with playing the race card: If everything is racist, nothing is racist. All of us know there are still racial issues that need to be dealt with in America and around the world, but the true issues get lost in the avalanche of unwarranted accusations.

Marxism is deadly. In 1999, *The Black Book of Communism* endeavored to tabulate a Marxist-Leninist death toll. It revealed 20 million deaths in the USSR, 65 million deaths in China, 1 million deaths in Vietnam, 2 million deaths in North Korea, 2 million deaths in Cambodia, 1 million deaths in Eastern Europe, 150,000 deaths in Latin America, and 1.7 million deaths in Ethiopia.

According to historian Paul Kengor, the death count that resulted from Marxism between 1917 and 1979 would "equate to a rate of multiple thousands of dead per day over the course of a century." World I and World War II would need to be combined and doubled to get near communism's butcher bill.[2] Aleksandr Solzhenitsyn taught that "socialism of any type and shade leads to a total destruction of the human spirit and to a leveling of mankind."

What Does This Mean?

This new political trajectory in our nation is more than just a trend. It is a seismic shift toward a Marxist agenda. We are harvesting the weeds from Karl Marx's toxic garden. If we look closely, we can draw the connections.

The Destruction of Monuments

It's become common in recent years to see videos of protesters defacing and removing statues and monuments they consider to be offensive. When we witness these events, we're seeing a concerted effort to attack and ultimately erase the past.

The word *remember* is found 164 times in the Old Testament. "Remember the former things of old," God said through the prophet Isaiah, "for I am God, and there is none like Me" (46:9). On the basis of past mercies, we can build a future of grace. We can say with the psalmist, "For You, O God, have . . . given me the heritage of those who fear Your name" (Psalm 61:5).

Biblical heroes built monuments to remind future generations of God's goodness and guidance. When God parted the waters of the Jordan River, Joshua said, "When your children ask their fathers in time to come, saying, 'What are these stones?' then you shall let your children know, saying, 'Israel crossed over this Jordan on dry land'" (Joshua 4:21–22).

Psalm 77:11 says, "Surely I will remember Your wonders of old." But revisionist historians are scrubbing our children's textbooks of all that is biblical or Christian, and they are rewriting our history to suit their own secular and socialist agendas.

Cancel Culture

In cultural Marxism, there can be no room for tolerance or dissenting opinions. Dreher wrote, "Today in our societies, dissenters . . . find their businesses, careers, and reputations destroyed. They are pushed out of the public square, stigmatized, canceled, and demonized as racists, sexists, homophobes and the like. And they are afraid to resist, because they are confident that no one will join them or defend them."[3]

Before the First Amendment is ushered out the door, let's reflect on what it says: "Congress shall make no law respecting an establishment of religion, or prohibiting the free exercise thereof; or abridging the freedom of speech, or of the press; of the right of the people peaceably to assemble, and to petition the Government for a redress of grievances."

The Dismantling of the Nuclear Family

Families based on Judeo-Christian values bred inequality, Marx thought. As Erwin Lutzer put it, "In Marxism, the family is perceived as a unit in which wives are suppressed by their husbands and children are suppressed by their parents."[4]

But God created the family. When God desired to create humanity, He created a family through Adam and Eve. Similarly, when God desired to reveal Himself more intimately to humanity, He spoke through Abraham's family. And when God chose to take on human flesh, He joined a family through the virgin birth. Socialists know that as long as the family remains strong, socialism cannot flourish. So, there's an ongoing attempt to subjugate the home to the government.

The Redistribution of Wealth

This ideology also teaches that all human assets should be claimed by the government and redistributed to the masses by a more equitable formula. But it doesn't take a scholar to see that wherever this principle has been implemented, the poor have gotten poorer and the few elitists who have been assigned to redistribute the wealth have themselves become filthy rich. Equality cannot be engineered. Iain Murray says, "The poor do the best in economically free societies and do the worst in societies where they are controlled in one way or another."[5]

Jude Dougherty, dean emeritus of the school of philosophy at Catholic University, understood the impossibility of universal equality when he wrote these words: "Men differ in strength, intelligence, ambition, courage, perseverance and all else that makes for success. There is no method to make men both free and equal."[6]

Defunding the Police

Socialists are especially keen on keeping the reins of law enforcement in their fists. They villainize the police, then defund them. Each city that slashed their police budget saw a dramatic uptick in violent crimes in the months that followed.

Unless something changes, our once beautiful cities will become wastelands where gangs rule the streets while progressive politicians go to and from work in their limousines accompanied by their expensive security personnel.

Paul called law enforcement "God's minister to you for good" (Romans 13:4). Without them our society would not be viable. The Lord views them as His ministers to maintain order on earth. In contrast, the socialist's motivation for vilifying local authorities is to let the local government fail so that they can federalize our cities and states, moving all power to Washington.

Where Do We Go From Here?

If we stopped the lesson at this point, we'd all be pretty grim. But darkness cannot withstand light, and Marxism is no match for the Master. Our Lord Jesus Christ "has gone into heaven and is at the right hand of God, angels and authorities and powers having been made subject to Him" (1 Peter 3:22).

Review What the Bible Says

First, we have to grasp what the Lord has to say about Marxist issues. Dr. Albert Mohler gives us a well-considered summary: "Scripture affirms the dignity of work (Ephesians 4:28) and the fact that those who refuse to work should not eat (2 Thessalonians 3:10). The Bible clearly affirms private property (Exodus 22:7) and condemns theft (Exodus 20:15) and covetousness (Exodus 20:17). Saving (Proverbs 13:22), thrift (Proverbs 21:20), land ownership (Acts 4:34–37), and investment (Matthew 25:27) are all honored in Scripture, and the Bible teaches that the laborer is worthy of his wages (Luke 10:7). Socialism contradicts or subverts every one of these principles."[7]

The Bible views personal property as a human right, telling us not to steal from one another (Exodus 20:15). It tells us the family, not the government, should provide primary care for one another (1 Timothy 5:8).

The Bible values industry and hard work (2 Thessalonians 3:10), and it warns against atheistic governmental systems (Romans 13:1).

Refuse to Live by Lies

We must also remain true to the truth. Proverbs 29:12 says, "If a ruler pays attention to lies, all his servants become wicked."

After his expulsion from Russia for writing his famous work, *Gulag Archipelago*, Aleksandr Solzhenitsyn published a final message to the Russian people: "Live Not By Lies." Christians, too, have been called to refuse falsehood—even to accept or listen to what is false. "Lying lips are an abomination to the LORD," wrote Solomon (Proverbs 12:22). "He who works deceit shall not dwell within my house," echoed the psalmist. "He who tells lies shall not continue in my presence" (Psalm 101:7).

So much of what we hear in our culture today has no connection to common sense, and it often feels easier just to ignore the falsehoods and mistruths. But ignoring them allows those falsehoods to continue. Even to thrive! Instead, let us refuse to live by lies.

Resolve to Follow Christ and Not Just Admire Him

Jesus said, "If you were of the world, the world would love its own. Yet because you are not of the world, but I chose you out of the world, therefore the world hates you" (John 15:19).

Since we are not of this world but chosen out of the world, everything about us should be under the King's control. It is God—not the government—that orders our lives. To persevere in an increasingly socialist culture, we have to decide whether to be Christ followers or merely Christ admirers.

This is what Jesus was talking about when He told us the cost of discipleship: "If anyone comes to Me and does not hate his father and mother, wife and children, brothers and sisters, yes, and his own life also, he cannot be My disciple. . . . So likewise, whoever of you does not forsake all that he has cannot be My disciple" (Luke 14:26, 33). It's our turn to put these words into practice.

Rethink Small Groups

Today's evolving political culture also compels us to upgrade all the small-group ministries in our churches. Small groups are vital in rough times.

Going back to the second chapter of Acts, let's remember the form established for us by the Early Church: "So continuing daily with one accord in the temple, and breaking bread from house to house, they ate their food with gladness and simplicity of heart, praising God" (Acts 2:46–47).

Small groups are gatherings that help us care for one another, study the instructions of Scripture, cope with the world, and advance with the gospel. They are biblical in nature, and they will prepare us to resist the socialist thought army that is surely coming after us.

Resist Any Way You Can

Let's remember Peter's words in Acts 5:29: "We ought to obey God rather than men." Anytime the government tries to force us to violate our biblical beliefs, we have a responsibility to speak up. You might be surprised to learn how receptive some of our leaders are to a calm, but assertive, word on behalf of our religious liberty.

For example, Elizabeth Turner worked hard on her valedictorian speech for Hillsdale High School in Hillsdale, Michigan. She intentionally highlighted her faith in Jesus. School officials removed all references to religion in her speech, but after an outpouring of support from Christians all over the country, the officials relented and promised that all future references to religion would be protected in speeches. Everyone's voice played a part, and this is an example of the power of our voices speaking up.

Remember Venezuela

Finally, remember Venezuela. A country once defined by freedom and opportunity is now oppressed, barren, and hopeless. That is the fruit of a Marxist revolution. Marxism is among the worst ideas ever conceived. We should be aware of its history, herald its dangers, and oppose its spread.

The best news of all is this: When Jesus returns, "the government will be upon His shoulder. . . . Of the increase of His government and peace there will be no end, upon the throne of David and over His kingdom, to order it and establish it with judgment and justice from that time forward, even forever" (Isaiah 9:6–7). Our Lord will "judge between the nations, and rebuke many people; they shall beat their swords into plowshares, and their spears into pruning hooks; nation shall not lift up sword against nation, neither shall they learn war anymore" (Isaiah 2:4).

When the twelve spies explored the Promised Land, only two of them brought back a faithful report: Joshua and Caleb. It was Caleb who later said: "And I brought [Moses] back a report according to my convictions" (Joshua 14:7, NIV). It's time for us all to live by convictions, not by convenience. And remember, the battle is the Lord's, and the truth cannot be intimidated.

APPLICATION

Personal Questions

1. Read Isaiah 9:6–7.

   a. What does this prophecy promise about the future of government? How does it differ from the current state of government in the world?

   b. How is this encouraging to the Christian currently struggling against the powers of this world?

   c. What does Isaiah say the government will be established with?

d. In what ways are the current governmental systems failing to operate in this way?

2. Read Joshua 14:7.

a. What did Caleb say his report was based on?

b. What are some ways that you can better live according to your convictions like Caleb did?

3. Read Acts 5:25–29.

a. What did Peter and the apostles tell the leaders of the Sanhedrin?

b. Who had told them to stop preaching in the name of Jesus?

c. What was the apostles' response?

d. How does that relate to you as you face increased pressure from governmental bodies to stop professing your faith in Christ?

e. What is one concept you can take away from these verses to hold onto in the midst of oppression?

Group Questions

1. Read John 15:18–25 together.

   a. What does Jesus say the world did to Him first in verse 18?

   b. What does Jesus say about our relationship to Him in verse 19?

   c. How can we expect to be treated based on this passage?

   d. What strength can we draw from this passage as we anticipate the hostility of the world and choose to follow Jesus anyway?

2. Read Acts 2:42–46 as a group.

    a. What did the apostles devote themselves to (verse 42)?

    b. How different does that look from what we experience in our churches?

    c. What can we do to make our churches look more like this and reflect Christ better?

    d. With what attitude did they do all this (verse 46)?

    e. How can we hold each other accountable to fellowship like this going forward?

3. Read 1 Peter 3:22 together.

    a. Where does this passage say Jesus now sits?

b. How does this passage comfort us as we struggle in this world?

c. Who does this passage say is subject to Jesus?

d. What boldness should that give us as we go about our weeks seeking to glorify God and reflect Him in all that we do?

DID YOU KNOW?

Socialism is a broad concept that is not easily defined. In fact, many so-called supporters of socialism are not even aware of what exactly they support. A YouGov survey found that 44 percent of Americans aged 16 to 29 supported socialism, but only one-third of the respondents could correctly identify what socialism was.[8] Many young Americans are enamored with the socialist ideals of Scandinavian countries while not realizing that private ownership of major industries is supported in those countries. Many people find what they want in some form of socialism without understanding its full scope or its historical failure.

Notes
1. Rod Dreher, *Live Not by Lies: A Manual for Christian Dissidents* (New York: Sentinel, 2020), 8.
2. Paul Kengor, *The Devil and Karl Marx: Communism's Long March of Death, Deception, and Infiltration* (Gastonia, NC: TAN Books, 2020), xix.

3. Rod Dreher, *Live Not by Lies: A Manual for Christian Dissidents* (New York: Sentinel, 2020), 8.
4. Erwin Lutzer, *We Will Not Be Silenced: Responding Courageously to Our Culture's Assault on Christianity* (Eugene, OR: Harvest House, 2020), 23.
5. Iain Murray, quoted in "The Temptations of Socialism: A Conversation With Economist Iain Murray," interview by Albert Mohler, February 1, 2021, https://albertmohler.com/2021/02/01/iain-murray.
6. Patrick J. Buchanan, *Suicide of a Superpower* (New York: Thomas Dunne, 2011), 207.
7. Albert Mohler, "The Coming Socialist Storm," *Decision Magazine*, January 1, 2021, https://decisionmagazine.com/albert-mohler-the-coming-socialist-storm/.
8. "Daily Survey: Socialism," *YouGov*, https://d25d2506sfb94s.cloudfront.net/cumulus_uploads/document/0ltegcolu7/tabs_YG_Socialism_20180801.pdf.

LESSON 2

AN INTERNATIONAL PROPHECY—
GLOBALISM

REVELATION 13:3

*In this lesson we learn about globalism, an increasingly
prevalent development in today's society that is predicted
in multiple biblical prophecies.*

Globalism—the worldwide interconnectedness of finance, trade, technology, and government—is an increasingly prevalent movement. After all, wouldn't the world run more smoothly if every country were interconnected and interdependent? But this is a dangerous philosophy because the book of Revelation predicts the rise of a one-world order ultimately led by the Antichrist. It is crucial we understand what globalism truly means and how it affects our future.

OUTLINE

I. What Does This Mean?
   A. What to Know About the Course of History
   B. What to Know About the Climax of History
   C. What to Know About the Culmination of History

II. Where Do We Go From Here?
  A. Worship Your Glorified Christ
  B. Embrace Your Global Mission
  C. Anticipate Your Glorious Hope

OVERVIEW

A treacherous storm is brewing in the world today: the waters of globalization, global governance, and a global economy. Even at this moment, we've already got our toes in those waters. In his book *The Ages of Globalization*, Jeffrey D. Sachs explains the world has been moving in stages toward a more globalized society from the past to the present day:

- *The Paleolithic Age*, which included small groups engaging in long-distance migration;
- *The Neolithic Age*, when humans became more adept at cultivating crops and began to trade with those in other places;
- *The Equestrian Age*, when people tamed the horse, allowing them to travel rapidly over longer distances;
- *The Classical Age* (1000 BC to AD 1500), which involved the rise and competition of large empires and their marching armies;
- *The Ocean Age* (1500 to 1800), when oceangoing navigation allowed transoceanic trade and naval warfare to colonize much of the world;
- *The Industrial Age* (1800 to 2000), which was characterized by accelerated science and technology, impacting the entire world; and
- *The Digital Age* (2000 to the present), which has "globalized economics and politics more directly and urgently" than ever before.[1]

Globalization is exactly what it sounds like—the global spread of finance, trade, technology, resources of all sorts, movements of all kinds, information, and people. It's the entire world bound up in interconnected systems. The world has been getting smaller with each passing era, its interconnectedness greater, and its inhabitants more vulnerable to a one-world government, given the right conditions. It's all in keeping with the predictions of Scripture.

What Does This Mean?

The more we become aware of this larger push toward globalization, the more frustrated we feel as average citizens. We're being swept along by forces beyond our control, forces that care little for our consent. At times, the relentless surge can be terrifying. Yet when we look at all of this from the biblical perspective, it takes away our fear and frustration. Almighty God has a predetermined plan for the history of His planet and its inhabitants. He's moving toward a day soon when "the earth will be filled with the knowledge of the glory of the LORD, as the waters cover the sea" (Habakkuk 2:14). The psalmist spoke of a time when "the whole earth [will] be filled with His glory" (Psalm 72:19). The book of Revelation predicts a time when "the kingdoms of this world" will become "the kingdoms of our Lord and of His Christ" (Revelation 11:15). Let's take a look at how we can grasp the broader scope of historical events—past, present, and future.

What to Know About the Course of History

The first attempt at globalization occurred in Genesis 11, when a powerful warlord named Nimrod established the empire of Babylon and built the Tower of Babel. He became the first global tyrant and began the dynasty that was later led by King Nebuchadnezzar, the most powerful man on earth in his day. In the heart of King Nebuchadnezzar's city rose a temple that was a new version of the Tower of Babel. Daniel was taken to the royal palace when Babylon conquered Daniel's homeland of Judah. "No wise man, enchanter, magician or diviner can explain to the king the mystery he has asked about," said Daniel without fear, "but there is a God in heaven who reveals mysteries. He has shown King Nebuchadnezzar what will happen in days to come" (Daniel 2:27-28, NIV).

In his dream, Nebuchadnezzar saw a massive statue, struck by a rock that was quarried by an invisible hand. The statue toppled and broke into a million bits that were swept away by the wind like chaff. The rock grew to become a mountain large enough to cover the entire earth. The interpretation is given in the last part of Daniel 2: The head of gold represented the empire of Babylon; the chest of silver, the next great world empire (Medo-Persia); the stomach and thighs of bronze, the next stage in world history (the Greek Empire of Alexander the Great). And the legs of iron symbolized the Roman Empire. The feet and toes of the statue represented a final coming world empire, that of the Antichrist. Jesus is the rock who will demolish history at its zenith and establish a truly global kingdom marked by righteousness and peace.

In the days of Nimrod, God broke up the globalization of his empire by confusing the languages. Under all these predicted governments, there was a sort of globalization. But after the fall of Rome, no single nation or empire has dominated the world. However, according to Daniel, there will be a final attempt in the future at a one-world government. It will be something of a revival of the Roman Empire made up of a confederation of ten kings or kingdoms, dominated by a Nimrod-type dictator and brought to an end with the Second Coming of Jesus Christ. "In the time of those kings, the God of heaven will set up a kingdom that will never be destroyed, nor will it be left to another people. It will crush all those kingdoms and bring them to an end, but it will itself endure forever" (Daniel 2:44, NIV).

What to Know About the Climax of History

As we just saw, there will be this final horrific attempt at manmade globalization before Jesus establishes His global Millennial Kingdom. This attempt will lead to a time of unprecedented and great tribulation. The book of Revelation completes the story begun by the book of Daniel. In Revelation 13, we're told that during days of great worldwide distress, Satan will raise up a man of lawlessness who will become the ultimate Nimrod. He's described in Revelation 13:1 as "a beast."

This chapter gives us the concluding picture of human globalization: "The whole world was filled with wonder and followed the beast. . . . The beast was given a mouth to utter proud words and blasphemies and to exercise its authority for forty-two months. . . . All inhabitants of the earth will worship the beast—all whose names have not been written in the Lamb's book of life" (Revelation 13:3–8, NIV). This Antichrist will rebuild the ancient city of Babylon for his world capital (Revelation 14:8) and will be on the verge of uniting the armies of the world in a last great attempt to destroy God's chosen nation of Israel. He will also globalize the economy, forcing everyone to be chipped in some way with his mark—the mysterious 666 of Revelation 13:18. Without this mark, no one will be able to make purchases or engage in commerce. Zechariah 12:3 speaks of a day when "all nations of the earth are gathered against [Jerusalem]."

That is when Christ will return—like a rock that strikes the edifice of world history and sends it shattering into the wind. Christ will then establish His own global kingdom. The Bible says, "For the mystery of lawlessness is already at work; only He who now restrains will do so until He is taken out of the way. And then the lawless one will be revealed, whom the Lord will consume with the breath of His mouth and destroy with the brightness of His coming" (2 Thessalonians 2:7-8). This is the climax of human history, when Christ will come again as a conqueror on a white horse followed by armies of heaven (Revelation 19:11-16). Zechariah said: "I will gather all the nations to Jerusalem to fight against it. . . . Then the LORD will go out and fight against those nations, as he fights on a day of battle. On that day his feet will stand on the Mount of Olives. . . . The LORD will be king over the whole earth. On that day there will be one LORD, and his name the only name" (Zechariah 14:2-9, NIV).

What to Know About the Culmination of History

This coming kingdom is what we often call the Millennium, based on the teaching in Revelation 20 that the earthly reign of Christ will last one thousand years. All the world will see globalization at its finest—under the Lord Jesus Christ! During the coming global reign of Christ, Jerusalem will be the capital of the earth, and people from all the nations will regularly come to visit, learn, and worship (Isaiah 2:2-3). The Millennial temple in Jerusalem will be the most beautiful building on earth (Ezekiel 40), and it will be filled with the glory of the Lord (Ezekiel 43). The Lord Jesus will be the ultimate international diplomat, negotiating peace treaties between rival nations (Isaiah 2:4). He will bring peace to the earth and wars will cease (Isaiah 2:4). He will occupy the ancient throne of His forefather, David (Luke 1:32-33).

The people of earth will travel to Jerusalem on a regular basis to worship the King and to keep the feasts of Israel (Zechariah 14:16). The agriculture of earth will be so improved that the reapers will have a hard time staying ahead of the sowers. The grain and grapes will grow so fast they can hardly be harvested (Amos 9:13). The deserts will become as green as lush mountains (Isaiah 35:2). Life expectancy will rival the lifespans of the days before the Great Flood, when people lived to be hundreds of years old (Isaiah 65:20). Nature will be transformed so that wolves and lambs will graze side by side, as will lions and cows (Isaiah 11:7; 65:25).

Songs of praise will ascend from the ends of the earth (Isaiah 24:16), and joy will cover the world (Isaiah 35:10). This is a *prelude* to heaven. Isaiah summed it up when he said: "Nothing will hurt or destroy in all my holy mountain, for as the waters fill the sea, so the earth will be filled with people who know the LORD" (Isaiah 11:9, NLT). After the thousand-year reign of Christ, earth's history will be over. The old universe will melt away, and God's children will be ushered into the new heavens, the new earth, and the celestial city of New Jerusalem.

Where Do We Go From Here?

If the future of our planet is globalized terror under the Antichrist followed by a glorious thousand-year reign of Christ, how should we then live? Jesus, during His ascension, gives this answer: "When they had come together, they asked Him, saying, 'Lord, will You at this time restore the kingdom to Israel?' And He said to them, 'It is not for you to know times or seasons which the Father has put in His own authority. But you shall receive power when the Holy Spirit has come upon you; and you shall be witnesses to Me in Jerusalem, and in all Judea and Samaria, and to the end of the earth.' . . . And while they looked steadfastly toward heaven as He went up, behold, two men stood by them in white apparel, who also said, 'Men of Galilee, why do you stand gazing up into heaven? This same Jesus, who was taken up from you into heaven, will so come in like manner as you saw Him go into heaven'" (Acts 1:6–11). In light of this passage, here are three concrete ways we can respond today to the Good News of tomorrow.

Worship Your Glorified Christ

Jesus ascended and resumed His place at the right hand of the Father. One of the disciples who saw Jesus ascend into the clouds was the apostle John. He later described the enthroned Christ as "the Son of Man, clothed with a garment down to the feet and girded about the chest with a golden band.

His head and hair were white like wool, as white as snow, and His eyes like a flame of fire" (Revelation 1:13–14).

The same Jesus who walked the dusty roads of Galilee now presides over the affairs of the universe and the annals of history. In uncertain times, we can either worry about the headlines or we can worship Him who is Head over all. Just as the disciples gazed into heaven, astounded at their ascended Lord, we should do the same. From childhood to old age, a life of praise is a life of peace, for when our eyes are on Jesus Christ, we know it is well with our souls.

Embrace Your Global Mission

The disciples didn't stay in that spot gazing into heaven all day. They returned to Jerusalem to prepare for something new—the global mission of the gospel. As never before in human history, we have an opportunity to take the gospel to every town, every tribe, and every tongue. Dr. Albert Mohler wrote, "The church of the Lord Jesus Christ understands global mission as a command and as a mandate from the Lord. While the world may debate globalization in terms of its economic and sociological effects, the church must see globalization as an unprecedented opportunity. Globalization may be a surprise to sociologists, politicians, and businessmen, but it comes as a great promise to followers of the Lord Jesus Christ. The current generation of Christians has unprecedented opportunities to proclaim the name of Jesus in all of the world and to see people of all tribes, tongues, and nations bow the knee to the King."[2] Since we live in a globalized world, we've never had more potential in reaching the globe for Christ. As long as Christ tarries, we must keep going to our cities, states, nations, and to the uttermost parts of the world.

Anticipate Your Glorious Hope

Finally, we should always anticipate our glorious hope. In Acts 1, Jesus had no sooner disappeared into a bright cloud of glory than two angels appeared. They must have been hurtling down from heaven as Jesus was rocketing up. They said to the disciples, "Men of Galilee, why do you stand gazing up into heaven? This same Jesus, who was taken up from you into heaven, will so come in like manner as you saw Him go into heaven" (Acts 1:11). From that point, every hero in the New Testament began looking for and longing for the return of Christ. Paul said, "There is laid up for me the crown of righteousness, which the Lord, the righteous Judge, will give to me on that Day, and not to me only but also to all who have loved His appearing" (2 Timothy 4:8). Peter said, "But in keeping with his promise we are looking forward to a new heaven and a new earth, where righteousness dwells" (2 Peter 3:13, NIV). John wrote, "We shall be like Him, for we shall see Him as He is" (1 John 3:2).

We should actively contemplate and anticipate the imminent return of Jesus, even as humanity continues its push toward a destructive version of globalization. Paul explained, God has scattered people and set their boundaries "so that they should seek the Lord, in the hope that they might grope for Him and find Him" (Acts 17:27). Christ will appear just as He ascended, and He will establish a global kingdom to show us how things should have always been. In the meantime, let's worship Him every day, speed the gospel on its way to the ends of the earth, and look forward to His soon and swift return!

APPLICATION

Personal Questions

1. Read Daniel 2:24–45. Look at the imagery of the "great image" and Daniel's interpretation of it.

   a. What are the various parts listed in King Nebuchadnezzar's dream?

   b. In a sentence, what was Daniel's core interpretation of the king's dream?

c. Why are the feet and the rock significant, and how is this important for you?

d. With what attitude and words did Daniel approach the king's throne? How can you have the same boldness as Daniel in your daily life?

2. Read Isaiah 2:1–4.

a. Where does Isaiah say the Lord's house will be established (verse 2)?

b. What does Isaiah say God will do for those who come to God (verse 3)?

c. From where will the law and the Word of God come from in the days prophesied by Isaiah (verse 3)?

d. What will God's rebuke cause the people of the world to do? What does this tell you about what happens when you obey God and listen to His Word (verse 4)?

3. Read Acts 1:1–11. Imagine you were there on the scene. How would you have felt? Would you have been reluctant to leave? Why did the disciples go back into the city, and what do their actions mean to you today?

Group Questions

1. Read Acts 1:6–11. Pay special attention to the commands given by Jesus to the disciples.

   a. What are we called to do while we await the return of Jesus (verse 8)?

   b. By whose authority do we witness? What does this do for our confidence as we share God's gift of salvation (verse 8)?

   c. What did the angels say to the onlooking disciples (verse 11)? How is this relevant to us as we study God's Word?

2. Read Acts 17:22–34. In the lesson, we saw a statement Paul made about globalization in his sermon on Mars Hill.

   a. What had the Athenians been worshiping when Paul came to them?

   b. What does this say about the spiritual state of people who are not believers, and how can we be aware of this when we are witnessing to them?

   c. What does Paul say about seeking the Lord? Why is it important that he said God is "not far from each one of us" (verse 27)?

   d. How does Paul's approach in Athens motivate us to be bold in sharing the gospel? What concrete steps can you take to share your faith this week? Discuss as a group.

DID YOU KNOW?

King Nebuchadnezzar of the Babylonian Empire was the most powerful ruler of his day, possibly the most powerful ruler ever up to that point. His empire reached from the Black Sea to the Mediterranean Sea to the Persian Gulf. When Iraqi dictator Saddam Hussein came to power in the same land that had once been ruled by Nebuchadnezzar, he is reported to have believed that he was a reincarnation of Nebuchadnezzar, rising up to once again make a name for Babylon and increase its military might.

Notes

1. Jeffrey D. Sachs, *The Ages of Globalization* (New York: Columbia University Press, 2020), xiii.
2. Albert Mohler, "Globalization and the Christian Mission," *Tabletalk*, November 2017, https://tabletalkmagazine.com/article/2017/11/globalization-christian-mission/.

LESSON 3

A BIOLOGICAL PROPHECY— PANDEMIC

MATTHEW 24:7

In this lesson we learn that events like pandemics can create uncertainty, but they teach us to pray, serve others, count our blessings, stay calm, and then do the next thing.

The world changed on January 11, 2020, when the first COVID-19 death was reported in China. The pandemic shook our world and disrupted our lives, but it didn't surprise the Lord. In the Bible, the words *plague, pandemic, pestilence*, and *disease* occur many times. The book of Revelation warns of plagues and possible pandemics during the Tribulation. Perhaps we are seeing the foreshadowing of that now. We need to know what it means and where to go from here.

OUTLINE

I. What Does This Mean?
A. The Vulnerability of Us All
B. The Credibility of the Bible
C. The Uncertainty of Life
D. The Sufficiency of Jesus

II. Where Do We Go From Here?
    A. Prioritize Your Prayer Life
    B. Sacrificially Serve Others
    C. Count Your Blessings
    D. Stay Calm and Carry On
    E. Do the Next Right Thing

OVERVIEW

Many of us learned during the COVID-19 pandemic to trust God as we had never before experienced. How thankful we are to have a trustworthy God! If we're followers of Christ, we don't have to live at the mercy of present problems and future fears. Instead, we can evaluate global events in terms of scriptural prophecy.

The English word *pandemic* didn't show up in dictionaries until 1853. The Latin prefix *pan* means "all." The root term *demic* comes from the word *demotic*, from which we get *democracy*. It means "belonging to the people." A pandemic involves the whole population of earth. Not every use of *pestilence, plague,* and *disease* in Scripture refers to a pandemic of infectious illness. But many of those references do. Throughout the Bible, we see repeated examples of God using diseases to accomplish His divine purposes. In Exodus 9, the Lord allowed an infectious skin disease to sweep over Egypt. When King David sinned against Israel, the Lord "sent a plague upon Israel from the morning till the appointed time" (2 Samuel 24:15).

This isn't to say that all illnesses are God initiated or that He sent COVID-19 to the earth. We live in a world corrupted by sin, and diseases of all kinds are a consequence of that corruption. Still, the Lord is not ignorant of what's happening on our globe.

In the Gospels, Jesus warned His disciples that "pestilences" will be one of the signs of the Last Days. These ravaging illnesses will shake the world, seeking to awaken people to the imminence of Christ's return to judge and reign (Matthew 24:7).

In Revelation, the Lord warned a dozen times about terrible pestilences and plagues coming to the nations as part of His judgment prior to the

Second Coming. This period is known as the Great Tribulation (Revelation 7:14), the most devastating period of divine judgment in human history. It will include plagues.

What Does This Mean?

What does all this mean? The COVID-19 pandemic feels like something we've read about in the Bible. After all, it's the most apocalyptic thing that has ever happened to most of us. Does COVID-19 mean anything when set against the larger scale of history? And if so, what?

During the last week of His life, the Lord Jesus left the temple in Jerusalem with His disciples, hiked down the Kidron Valley, and climbed to the top of the Mount of Olives. The disciples asked Jesus about the Last Days, prompting our Lord's most comprehensive teaching on the events related to the end of the world and His glorious return. We call this the Olivet Discourse. Jesus said, "And there will be famines, pestilences, and earthquakes in various places. All these are the beginning of sorrows" (Matthew 24:7-8).

In Matthew 24:1-14, Jesus warned of six things that would happen as His Second Coming began to draw near: (1) deception by false Christs (verses 4-5); (2) disputes and warfare among nations (verses 6-7); (3) disease and famine worldwide (verses 7-8); (4) deliverance of believers to tribulation (verses 9); (5) defection of false believers (verses 10-13); and (6) declaration of the gospel to the whole world (verse 14).

These six signs cover the first three and one-half years of the Tribulation period and coincide with the prophecies in Revelation. But while these signs will be fulfilled during the Tribulation period, they will not start just then. They will build up over time. Perhaps we're seeing early evidence of these signs.

The Bible predicts the return of Christ for His Church at any moment. This event is known as the Rapture. Following the Rapture of the Church, there will be seven years of global Tribulation. These are described in detail in Revelation 6-18. The last half of this seven-year period will be known as the Great Tribulation and will be a unique outpouring of God's wrath on the earth as the world hurtles toward Armageddon. When that period concludes, Jesus will return with His Church to put an end to global conflicts and pandemics, to judge evil, and to establish His thousand-year kingdom. His return is described in Revelation 19.

So there are no events predicting the Rapture, but the signs point to His return. Why, then, should we be concerned about signs? Because future events cast their shadows before them! God's people should be Bible students. Bible students should be interested in prophetic passages. And when we study those prophetic passages, we should learn to spot the signs of the times, because we can often see trends and patterns emerging.

Is, then, this COVID-19 pandemic a sign of the Second Coming of Christ? Possibly. It could be an early indication of number three on Jesus' list of signs—disease and famine worldwide. Some of the Tribulation signs could spill over into the final years before the Rapture. Jesus said this "pestilence" would arrive like "birth pains" (Matthew 24:8, NIV). This means it will increase in frequency and intensity in the time leading up to His return. In other words, as the end approaches, we should expect infectious disease outbreaks to occur more frequently.

While the coronavirus may not perfectly qualify as a prophetic sign, it is nonetheless a sign. It's hard to see the world so convulsed by an event without looking at it through the lens of Scripture and learning its lessons. Even if COVID-19 is not a sign of the future, it is a sign for today—a reminder of things we too easily forget. How many people watched the headlines and felt as if a global storm was approaching!

The Vulnerability of Us All

First, events like coronavirus remind us we're all more vulnerable than we like to think. According to most reports, the elderly and those with an underlying health condition were the most vulnerable to the virus. But as time progressed, we discovered that everyone was vulnerable, including celebrities who think they live in a bubble. Doctors struggled to find a pattern as to why some people were in ICUs, while others simply lost their sense of taste and smell. Some older people weathered the virus without problems, while some teenagers found themselves struggling for life. Money can buy us a test, but it cannot buy us invincibility. We're all vulnerable to these super plagues. No one is safe. No one escapes the possibility of infection.

Often, we see in the news (and even in our daily lives) people acting as if they are invincible. But our vulnerability and mortality are brought to light by cataclysmic events like the COVID-19 pandemic, and we see the need for the great, immortal God in our mortal lives. The uncertainty of the pandemic leads us to seek knowledge that we cannot attain on our own; and the imperfections of our human form mean that we need something, and Someone, greater than ourselves. How blessed are we to have God Almighty's very words to guide and lead us to a greater calling in our lives!

The Credibility of the Bible

COVID-19 also tells us something about the credibility of Scripture. The events described in Revelation have never seemed so plausible as they seem now. These apocalyptic events appear to be knocking on the door.

Ezekiel predicted a coming war in which Russia and its coalition armies will try to destroy the nation of Israel in the early days of the Tribulation. These armies will be destroyed by monumental convulsions of the earth, by military confusion, by multiple calamities, and finally by major plagues. The Lord predicts, "I will bring him to judgment with pestilence and bloodshed" (Ezekiel 38:22). It will take seven months to bury the bodies (Ezekiel 39:12). Unburied bodies will undoubtedly cause a malignant plague. According to Ezekiel, God will summon vast flocks of birds to the Middle East to devour the bodies scattered across the land.

In Revelation 9:18, a third of the earth will perish by various plagues caused by demonic forces. In Revelation 11, the two supernatural witnesses will have power "to strike the earth with all plagues, as often as they desire" (verse 6). That warning isn't limited to pandemics, but neither does it exclude infectious diseases. In all these ways, the truth of the Bible is demonstrated as credible.

The Uncertainty of Life

Contagions also remind us of the uncertainty of life. No one expected to stay away from work, school, or church for a year. How terrible for those who were laid off or whose businesses failed. According to the apostle James, we should not be surprised by the unexpected: "You do not know what will happen tomorrow. For what is your life? It is even a vapor that appears for a little time and then vanishes away" (James 4:14). How uncertain and precious are our days! We must all find some quiet time to reflect on life and give thanks to God for the days and months and years He has given to us.

Job said, "Now my days are swifter than a runner; they flee away, they see no good. They pass by like swift ships, like an eagle swooping on its prey" (Job 9:25–26). He also added, "Man who is born of woman is of few days and full of trouble. He comes forth like a flower and fades away; he flees like a shadow and does not continue" (Job 14:1–2).

The Sufficiency of Jesus

The virus also points us to Jesus's sufficiency. Jesus said: "These things I have spoken to you, that in Me you may have peace. In the world you will have tribulation; but be of good cheer, I have overcome the world" (John 16:33). Notice the phrase "in Me." The Lord's promise to the disciples was the promise of Himself. His peace was to be found in Him! Jesus didn't say, "In the world you will have tribulation, but I have overcome *tribulation*." He said, "In the world you will have tribulation, but I have overcome the *world*." Jesus doesn't just overcome the event. He overcomes the environment in which the event occurs.

Jesus comes to us in the midst of the struggle, when the battle is almost unbearable and the circumstances look impossible. With the voice of absolute certainty and strength, He speaks to us of peace and bestows the encouragement we need. He raises our morale and fills us with strength. He says to us: "My peace I give to you; not as the world gives do I give to you. Let not your heart be troubled, neither let it be afraid" (John 14:27).

Where Do We Go From Here?

What about the possibility that COVID-19 is a sign of the End Times? Based on the things we've learned about biblical prophecy and the pandemic, what should we do now? How is the Lord calling us to action? Here are five suggestions on how Christians can continue to live for God during any present or future pandemic.

Prioritize Your Prayer Life

The first place to go is to the place of prayer. For that we have a great example in 2 Chronicles 20. King Jehoshaphat faced an existential crisis when multiple armies headed toward Judah. He responded with masterful spiritual leadership. He prayed, "If disaster comes upon us—sword, judgment, pestilence, or famine—we will stand before this temple and in Your presence (for Your name is in this temple), and cry out to You in our affliction, and You will hear and save" (2 Chronicles 20:9).

In verses 5–12, the king offered a model prayer. He appealed to God's character, His promises, and His actions in the past. The prayer ended with these superb words: "We have no power against this great multitude that is coming against us; nor do we know what to do, but our eyes are upon You" (2 Chronicles 20:12). We must appeal to God's character, confess our inability, and put our eyes on the Lord.

Sacrificially Serve Others

During the pandemic, we all found ways to serve others. Don't let that momentum come to an end just because we get back to "normal" life. Moments of danger present opportunities for service, but so do moments that are more mundane. Also, remember that as the physical needs of this current crisis come to a close, our nation and our world will still have myriad spiritual needs. We still have opportunities to serve!

As Martin Luther put it, "If you wish to serve Christ and to wait on Him, very well, you have your sick neighbor close at hand. Go to him and serve him, and you will surely find Christ in him." Luther was telling us something about serving Jesus by serving others. Remember when the Lord said, "Assuredly, I say to you, inasmuch as you did it to one of the least of these My brethren, you did it to Me" (Matthew 25:40). That's powerful to contemplate. Imagine coming across people this very day, seeing their needs, and thinking of them as if they were Christ! When we help someone else in His name, we are helping Him. That compels us to sacrificially serve others, even in crises like pandemics.

Count Your Blessings

Then what? We count our blessings. The Bible says, "From his abundance we have all received one gracious blessing after another" (John 1:16, NLT). Paul wrote, "Blessed be the God and Father of our Lord Jesus Christ, who has blessed us with every spiritual blessing in the heavenly places in Christ" (Ephesians 1:3). God has blessed us with every spiritual blessing in the heavenly places in Christ—period! In times like these, our blessings become clearer, richer, and more meaningful. Something happens deep in our hearts when we count those blessings. This helps us make spiritual progress in life.

The peripheral values that clutter our lives fall away when we are forced to slow down, and we can focus on existential issues and eternal blessings—the ones we overlook when we're too busy. Haven't you noticed how the simple blessings of life are often the best ones?

Stay Calm and Carry On

Gratitude will help us to stay calm and carry on, as the British said during World War II. The Bible teaches, "God has not given us a spirit of fear, but of power and of love and of a sound mind" (2 Timothy 1:7). The Lord created our human imagination to be a powerful force. It can create beautiful visions of a desirable future, or it can conjure up worst-case scenarios. These dark products of the imagination can put us in the grip of fear—a place God would never have us go. As this Scripture verse shows, the power that banishes fear is a sound mind. We maintain a sound mind by "bringing every thought into captivity to the obedience of Christ" (2 Corinthians 10:5).

Gaining a sound and centered mind is not as difficult as we think. If we simply read the Scriptures deeply, thoughtfully, and openly every day, we will invite the Holy Spirit to whisper new strength into our thoughts. He and He alone can tame the reckless power of the human mind. A mind centered on the truth of God is the key to His sustaining grace. He will keep us from losing heart. When we realize that Jesus is present today and will be present tomorrow, we can be set free from worry.

Do the Next Right Thing

Finally, we have to keep busy with whatever God assigns us day by day. During the pandemic, many people were frustrated when their routines vanished. We need to have meaningful activities for all our days. So we must learn the power of doing "the next right thing." The pandemic might change the type or intensity of our work, but as long as God keeps us on earth, He has jobs for us each day. Elisabeth Elliot found a poem about this:

Fear not tomorrows, child of the King,
Trust them with Jesus, do the next thing
Do it immediately, do it with prayer;
Do it reliantly, casting all care;
Do it with reverence, tracing His hand
Who placed it before thee with earnest command.
Stayed on Omnipotence, safe 'neath His wing,
Leave all results, do the next thing.

APPLICATION

Personal Questions

1. Read Matthew 24:1–14.

   a. What questions did the disciples ask Jesus on the Mount of Olives?

   b. What are some of the "signs of the times" that will point to our Lord's return?

   c. In verse 7, Jesus mentioned pestilences. How would you define this word? Do you think Jesus may have had an event like the COVID-19 pandemic in mind when He discussed pestilences?

2. Read Revelation 11:1–6. This passage predicts the appearance of two great and godly preachers during the Tribulation period.

   a. In verse 5, what will happen to those who oppose these two witnesses?

   b. In verse 6, what powers will these two witnesses wield to bring judgment?

3. In light of pandemic-like events, we must be faithful in prayer. Read 2 Chronicles 20:1–12.

   a. What can you learn from the prayer offered by King Jehoshaphat on this occasion?

   b. What message did God give him in return (verse 17)?

4. We also need to count our blessings, even in difficult times. What does Ephesians 1:3 say about the way God has blessed us?

5. Read 2 Timothy 1:7. What assurance does this verse give you during global or personal emergencies?

6. This lesson ended by suggesting we learn to always do the next right thing. For you, what would that be?

Group Questions

1. Read Matthew 24:1–14. Make a list of the signs of the times that Jesus describes in these verses.

2. While these signs will take place during the Tribulation, leading up to the return of Christ, we can see evidence of them in our world today. Which of these signs seems especially prominent? Which intrigues you the most?

3. Read Matthew 25:1–13, the parable of the ten virgins. This parable is part of the same sermon Jesus began in Matthew 24, which we call the Olivet Discourse. Summarize the lesson Jesus wants us to learn from this parable.

4. This lesson touched on how vulnerable we are to events outside our control and the uncertainty of life. What does James 4:14 say about this? Compare that with Psalm 78:39. Does this bother you? Why or why not?

5. In light of these things, it is important to prioritize our prayer lives. Read 2 Chronicles 20:1–12. What impresses you the most about King Jehoshaphat's prayer?

6. What does it mean, in practical terms, to count your blessings? In practical terms, how can you begin counting your blessings in your daily life?

7. Read 2 Timothy 1:7. What is the one attitude we should reject and the three attitudes we should embrace? What is the role of the Holy Spirit in this?

DID YOU KNOW?

As bad as COVID-19 was, the 1918 flu pandemic was more deadly. Between fifty and one hundred million people died, which represented 5 percent of the earth's population at that time. Many of these were young people, as soldiers from World War I returned to their homes all over the world, unaware they were carrying a deadly virus. The crowded conditions in military camps contributed to its spread. The 1918 pandemic is often called the Spanish Flu, but there is no reason to believe it originated in Spain. It sprang out of the European war with soldiers coming and going from many nations.

LESSON 4

A FINANCIAL PROPHECY— ECONOMIC CHAOS

REVELATION 13:17

*In this lesson we learn about the Antichrist and the False Prophet
who will rise up to dominate the global economy.*

The Antichrist will rise to power as a charismatic figure who will captivate the hearts of many, and the False Prophet will be at his right hand. Their influence on the global economy will turn into an unprecedented cult of the Beast that will force all of humanity to bear his mark to access commerce and employment, and it will ban believers who refuse the mark from all of the world's resources. This will intensify the persecution of Christians.

OUTLINE

I. **What Does This Mean?**
   A. The Addiction to Money
   B. The Acceleration of Inequality
   C. The Adoration of the Antichrist

II. **Where Do We Go From Here?**
   A. Determine to Count the Cost
   B. Determine to Be Confident
   C. Determine to Be Content

OVERVIEW

Much of the world's attention is devoted to its economy—the global world of finance. At any moment, there could be a coming economic Armageddon. Some of the most recent economic trends and technology may foreshadow the financial world of the Tribulation period. For example, the evolving biometric chip technology reminds us of a prophecy found in Revelation 13:16–17—a passage predicting something that will happen during the Great Tribulation: "He causes all . . . to receive a mark on their right hand or on their foreheads, and that no one may buy or sell except one who has the mark or the name of the beast." This technology is coming more quickly than we know. Imagine this technology in the wrong hands. Without being dogmatic or an alarmist, it feels like biometric chips could be a precursor of Revelation 13. We'll take a deeper look at that passage and its ramifications later in this lesson.

One more item deserves mention: the rise of all-digital currencies, also known as cryptocurrencies. Digital currencies are decentralized and exist entirely in the world of cyberspace. They are produced online, stored online, and spent online. The idea of government officials being able to access the financial records and transaction histories of ordinary citizens is frightening. More and more, people in the Western world are buying, selling, and giving, not with physical money—coins and bills—but through a series of touches on a small screen. What does all this mean for our future? How does this affect the followers of the Lamb today?

What Does This Mean?

As we've seen throughout these pages, it's difficult to make definitive statements about future events. There are so many variables at play. Even when we have general principles and prophecies from God's Word to guide us, we must be careful about turning those principles and prophecies into specific predictions about people, places, and events. But there's one thing we can say with confidence: Money will play an essential role in future events, including the End Times. Money has always been important in the past, and everything connected with economics is increasingly important today. It's driving our world. We can assume that money will remain important in the future; it will dominate our world even more in days to come. The Bible is rich with information on this topic. Specifically, Scripture reveals that money will have an impact on the End Times, both leading up to and during the period known as the Tribulation. Let's talk about three of the most important financial signs of the End Times.

The Addiction to Money

According to Scripture, people will become increasingly greedy in the Last Days. The Bible says: "But know this, that in the last days perilous times will come: For men will be . . . lovers of money" (2 Timothy 3:1–2). It's easy to think of Wall Street when we read those verses, but we must grapple with this personally. Paul said the End Times will be defined by rejecting what is good and running to embrace what is evil, much of which will be centered on an ever-increasing appetite for money and the things we can do with it. That matches what Paul had previously written to Timothy: "For the love of money is a root of all kinds of evil, for which some have strayed from the faith in their greediness, and pierced themselves through with many sorrows" (1 Timothy 6:10).

Listen to John Piper's words about this: "God deals in the currency of grace, not money. . . . Money is the currency of human resources. So, the heart that loves money is a heart that pins its hopes, and pursues its pleasures, and puts its trust in what human resources can offer. So, the love of money is virtually the same as faith in money—belief (trust, confidence, assurance) that money will meet your needs and make you happy."[1] Look around you! This is everywhere. Our addiction to wealth will only grow stronger as we approach the end of history. We have to guard against our own attraction toward materialism. Finding the right balance in terms of lifestyle is challenging and requires divine wisdom. Financial greed is imbedded within our culture, but it cannot become instilled within our character.

The Acceleration of Inequality

The Last Days will also see increasing inequality. The Tribulation is the coming seven-year period during which God will complete His discipline of Israel and fully bring His wrath to bear on the evil of the world. Revelation 6–18 describes this future period. In Revelation 6, we read about things that will occur near the beginning of the Tribulation, including this: "When He opened the third seal, I heard the third living creature say, 'Come and see.' So I looked, and behold, a black horse, and he who sat on it had a pair of scales in his hand. And I heard a voice in the midst of the four living creatures saying, 'A quart of wheat for a denarius, and three quarts of barley for a denarius; and do not harm the oil and the wine'" (verses 5–6).

This passage describes the third "seal" of judgment that will be unleashed during the Tribulation. It paints a picture of worldwide famine, forcing many into poverty, hunger, and despair. Alarmingly, verse 6 says a quart of wheat will sell for a denarius (a day's wages) during the Tribulation period. The New Living Translation puts it this way: "A loaf of wheat bread or three loaves of barley will cost a day's pay. And don't waste the olive oil and wine" (Revelation 6:6). Basic staples and supplies will be outrageously expensive, but not everyone will be affected equally. Oil and wine were more like luxury items primarily reserved for those with more resources. Those will still be available.

In short, the Tribulation will be a period of extreme economic inequality. Most people will struggle to find basic supplies to meet their needs. Yet a few—perhaps those who gave themselves most fully to an addiction to money prior to the Tribulation—will hoard great amounts of wealth for themselves. Once again, we see these tendencies displayed in today's world. We will continue to see even greater levels of inequality as we draw closer to the Tribulation.

The Adoration of the Antichrist

The Man of Lawlessness will be the personification of charisma. But the Bible gives a clearer glimpse of him, calling him a beast "rising up out of the sea" (Revelation 13:1). He'll rule alongside a second beast, this one "coming up out of the earth" (Revelation 13:11). This second beast is called the False Prophet. He will have one supreme duty—to point humanity toward the Antichrist, in antithesis to how the Holy Spirit points people toward Jesus

Christ. This beast "had two horns like a lamb and spoke like a dragon" (verse 11). He will appear like a meek and gentle lamb, when in reality he will have the heart of a destroyer. Satan will be the power behind it all. The Antichrist will be the political leader during the Tribulation, and the False Prophet will be his spiritual and economic leader. He'll be able to accomplish incredible things such as bringing the Antichrist back to life after a mortal wound and enabling an idolatrous image to speak.

The False Prophet will have supernatural and demonic influence, and he will be in charge of the world's economy: "He causes all, both small and great, rich and poor, free and slave, to receive a mark on their right hand or on their foreheads, and that no one may buy or sell except one who has the mark or the name of the beast, or the number of his name. Here is wisdom. Let him who has understanding calculate the number of the beast, for it is the number of a man: His number is 666" (Revelation 13:16–18). Without this mark, people will be unable to buy or sell anything.

The word for "mark" in first-century Greek was *charagma*. It was connected with the emperor of Rome, containing his name, effigy, and the year of his reign. It was also necessary for commerce, and it was required to validate legal documents. The mark of the Beast will indicate that the one wearing it is a worshiper of the Beast—someone who submits to his rule. Those who refuse that mark will be traitors. Even more frightening, Satan and the Antichrist will create a union between religion and economics during the Tribulation period with no room for freedom of worship, expression, or ideas. The Antichrist will be at the top of a one-world cult, with his False Prophet by his side. Their unbending law will be, "Worship me or die." And they will use economic pressures to flog those who resist them.

Where Do We Go From Here?

Technology already exists that makes all this sound plausible. We can well imagine the economic and religious union summed up by the mark of the Beast. Addiction to money is a legitimate problem in many cultures around the world. The existence of economic inequality is here, and the culture is ready for a cult-like figure to emerge. But we can be aware of these trends without being seized with alarm. As followers of Christ, we are children of God. We are chosen members of His kingdom. We are His disciples and His friends. We're part of the family, included among the holy people and the royal nation that's dedicated to changing the world through the gospel of Christ. So we should respond to apocalyptic danger with emphatic determination and timely wisdom. Here's how.

Determine to Count the Cost

In the Gospel of Luke, Jesus told a parable about counting the cost. He said, "For which of you, intending to build a tower, does not sit down first and count the cost, whether he has enough to finish it—lest, after he has laid the foundation, and is not able to finish, all who see it begin to mock him, saying, 'This man began to build and was not able to finish'?. . . So likewise, whoever of you does not forsake all that he has cannot be My disciple" (14:28–29, 33).

Following Jesus carries a cost. Throughout history, many Christians have paid that cost with their lives. Many of us in the West have likely paid a minimal cost to follow Christ. Yet our circumstances may change. At some point they *will* change, probably sooner rather than later. As the world veers further away from God's values and as time moves closer toward Armageddon, we'll arrive at a moment when proclaiming the name of Jesus requires a sacrifice.

But wouldn't we rather have Jesus than anything this world affords? Let's take this moment to count the cost, realistically but optimistically. We can place on one side of the scale all of the trappings of our riches, our possessions, our comfort, our career, and so on. On the other side of the scale, let's place the incredible, unthinkable blessing of eternal life in the presence of our Savior. As we make our own calculations and count our individual cost for following Christ, we'll say with the apostle Paul, "Oh, the depth of the riches both of the wisdom and knowledge of God!" (Romans 11:33).

Determine to Be Confident

The wonderful news about living for Jesus is that not only can we experience the riches of the wisdom and knowledge of God, but we can also feel confident in the reality of God's presence right now. No matter what cost we may pay to follow Christ, we will never sacrifice our connection to Him.

The author of Hebrews put it this way: "For He Himself has said, 'I will never leave you nor forsake you.' So we may boldly say: 'The Lord is my helper; I will not fear. What can man do to me?'" (13:5–6) This is one of the most emphatic statements in the New Testament. No matter what happens in your life, God will always be there. He will never abandon you! Rather than yielding to culture's continual cry for more, we can declare our confidence in God—and in Him alone. He is our Helper. He is our Sustainer, our Provider, and He will always be there.

As confident Christians, we stand in a place of security because we know God is enough for any and every situation we might face. David expressed this sentiment: "The LORD is my light and my salvation; whom shall I fear? The LORD is the strength of my life; of whom shall I be afraid?" (Psalm 27:1)

Since we have the Lord, we can never be left without a friend or a treasure or a dwelling place. This enables us to feel independent of the sinful desires of humanity and all its schemes. When we stand in such awe of the living Lord, the lying world loses its power on us. So don't fear. Even if our culture continues down a path of greed, we don't have to walk that path. Don't settle for anything less than the riches of God's goodness, love, mercy, and provision, which He can pour into our lives like rivers from heaven! Let's make up our minds to be confident in God, for the Bible says, "In quietness and confidence shall be your strength" (Isaiah 30:15).

Determine to Be Content

Finally, because God will never leave us nor forsake us, we can be content with what we have. The Bible can keep us from yielding to the pressure of the world's worship of money. Scripture teaches us how to distance ourselves from a materialistic lifestyle by developing the simple biblical attitude of contentment. Two passages instantly come to mind: "Let your conduct be without covetousness; be content with such things as you have" (Hebrews 13:5); and "He who loves silver will not be satisfied with silver; nor he who loves abundance, with increase. This also is vanity" (Ecclesiastes 5:10). Covetousness is subtle because it's a condition within our minds, causing people to agonize over, lust after, and be consumed by the desire to have what someone else has. It is an internal spiritual disease that, if not checked, will eventually manifest itself externally. The writer of Hebrews tells us how to replace coveting with contentment. The Greek word for *contentment* means "satisfied," "adequate," "competent," or "sufficient." The same term is used in 2 Corinthians 12:9, when God told Paul: "My grace is sufficient for you."

Someone has said, "Christian contentment is the God-given ability to be satisfied with the loving provision of God in any and every situation." According to Paul's epistle to the church in Philippi, contentment is something we learn. This is the apostle's own testimony: "Not that I speak in regard to need, for I have learned in whatever state I am, to be content: I know how to be abased, and I know how to abound. Everywhere and in all things I have learned both to be full and to be hungry, both to abound and to suffer need. I can do all things through Christ who strengthens me" (Philippians 4:11–13).

Paul wasn't born a saint. He didn't come into the world with a vast reserve of contentment. Instead, he learned contentment through experience—including both comfort and hardship. He learned contentment by honestly evaluating the value of wealth versus the value of his connection to Christ. And he learned contentment through the continual influx and influence of God's Spirit in his life. The same can be true for us. Yes, our world's approach to money is troubling. But we can avoid this danger in our culture. We must determine to count the cost (and the benefits!) of following Christ, choose to remain confident in His presence, and learn to be content with His provision in our lives. As someone said, "You can take the world, but give me Jesus!"

APPLICATION

Personal Questions

1. Read Revelation 13:1–10.

   a. Who gives the Beast his authority (verse 2)?

b. Who does that represent? Why is it important?

c. What happens to the Beast (verse 3)? How does this further his influence?

d. What did the lesson say about this, and how is it resolved? (For reference, see "The Adoration of the Antichrist" section.)

e. Why did the people referenced in Revelation worship the beast?

f. How can you use this passage as a warning against idolatry?

g. What will the Beast do to those on earth during his day (verse 7)?

h. How might this relate to you in the near future? What can you do to prepare for it?

i. How are some people saved from worshiping the Beast? What can you do this week to ensure that you are included among those people who do not worship him (verse 8)?

2. Have you seen echoes of this prophecy begin to appear in your own life right now?

3. What is the future downfall of the Beast (verse 10)? How can this serve as an encouragement to you as you meditate on this passage?

Group Questions

1. Read 2 Timothy 3.

   a. What kind of people are described at the beginning of this passage?

   b. What aspects of this description should we take as a warning as we go about our lives?

c. How did the people in this passage get to where they are?

d. What should our response be when we come across the influence of people like this (verse 5)?

e. In verse 7, what did Paul mean when he spoke of people ever learning but never coming to the "knowledge of the truth"? Where do you see this happening in our culture today?

f. Notice how Paul contrasts himself with the culture. What godly qualities did he boast about in verses 10–13?

g. What did he tell all of us to do in verses 14–17?

h. This is important as we face future times. What dangers will people face in Revelation 13:15–18?

i. How can we live a life free from materialist greed now?

2. What changes can you make in your life to live a life that's free from the love of money?

3. How can we hold each other accountable to live with less greed and covetousness? Discuss as a group.

DID YOU KNOW?

More and more people are having microchips inserted into their bodies in order to access their personal data and banking information. This is concerning for those who have read the book of Revelation. But for nonbelievers, microchips can be appealing. These implanted radio frequency identification (RFID) chips can turn people into "walking contactless smart cards" according to one BBC article.[2] This technology can be used to send text messages, wire money, operate computers, and purchase food. Recent updates to technology could even allow a person to unlock their houses, start their cars, and turn on their lights. While this technology is intriguing, it's also a definite cause for concern.

Notes

1. John Piper, "What It Means to Love Money," *Desiring God*, accessed May 24, 2021, https://www.desiringgod.org.
2. Richard Gray, "The Surprising Truths and Myths About Microchip Implants," *BBC*, August 2, 2017.

LESSON 5

A THEOLOGICAL PROPHECY— THE FALLING AWAY

2 THESSALONIANS 2:3

*In this lesson we learn that many apparent believers in Christ will
fall away from the faith before our Lord returns,
and we'll learn how to prevent such a thing from happening to us.*

Many Christians seem to take up the faith, only to fall away later. But this apostasy doesn't come as a surprise to seasoned Bible scholars because the Bible contains numerous teachings about the great "falling away" that will occur before the Second Coming of Jesus. We must be aware of this trend and oppose it. Even today, we're seeing more and more outward Christians turn away from the Lord and His Church. This is a sign of the hastening return of Christ. The Bible says, "Don't let anyone deceive you in any way. For that day will not come unless the apostasy comes first" (2 Thessalonians 2:3, CSB).

OUTLINE

I. What Does This Mean?

   A. Some Fall Away Because They Are Deceived

   B. Some Fall Away Because They Are Disillusioned

   C. Some Fall Away Because They Are Distracted

II. Where Do We Go From Here?
  A. Examine Yourselves
  B. Encourage Yourselves
  C. Exercise Yourselves

OVERVIEW

Many Christians seem to be falling away from the gospel. When Paul wrote to the Colossians and to Philemon, he sent greetings from his coworker, Demas, who was at his side (Colossians 4:14; Philemon 1:24). Yet in his final letter, Paul told Timothy, "Demas has forsaken me, having loved this present world" (2 Timothy 4:10). This sort of thing seems to be accelerating in our times. There are people who have, "trampled the Son of God underfoot . . . treated as an unholy thing the blood of the covenant that sanctified them, and . . . insulted the Spirit of grace" (Hebrews 10:29, NIV).

Another book in the Bible is devoted to this topic—the short epistle of Jude, written by our Lord's half-brother, the son of Joseph and Mary. It's the next-to-the-last book of the Bible, and Jude stated his purpose succinctly: "To contend earnestly for the faith which was once for all delivered to the saints" (verse 3). In only twenty-five verses, Jude reminds us that some of the angels themselves fell away from allegiance to God.

It helps me to realize the apostles faced the same problem of falling away we're seeing today. Yet the trend toward apostasy seems to be accelerating in our times. I'm almost hesitant to read Christian news sites because I don't want to hear of another pastor failing or another prominent believer rejecting the faith. Recent headlines aren't encouraging, and neither are the statistics. In the early 1980s, over 70 percent of Americans were church members. Now the number is about 47 percent.

But we shouldn't despair. There's hope. Hosea 14:4 says: "I will heal their apostasy; I will love them freely, for my anger has turned from them" (ESV).

What Does This Mean?

Apostasy is not the same thing as atheism. The word *apostasy* refers to people who had seemingly embraced Christianity only to fall away from the faith. Apostasy doesn't reflect the rise of atheism in and of itself, nor does it apply to everyone who chooses religious systems other than Christianity. Instead, the concept of falling away has a narrower focus. It applies specifically to apparent Christians—to those who claim to follow Jesus but then turn their backs on Him. Spiritual apostasy occurs when a person who once *claimed* to be a believer departs from what he formerly professed to believe. An apostate is not someone who was saved and then lost his or her salvation. It is someone who *claimed* to be a believer, never was, and then abandoned their profession.

This is a major theme of the book of Judges, which told the cyclical story of God's people falling away, repenting, and falling away again. The final verse of Judges offers a perfect summation of falling away: "In those days there was no king in Israel; everyone did what was right in his own eyes" (Judges 21:25). True apostasy means rejecting Jesus, our King, and choosing instead whatever seems right in our own eyes. Something similar happens with individual Christians who fall away from Christ; it happens by degrees. Over time, they find themselves drifting further from their relationship with Jesus until that relationship no longer carries any genuine meaning or life.

One of the signs of the imminent return of Christ is a rising number of self-proclaimed Christians who ultimately reject Christ. The Bible says, "Now, brethren, concerning the coming of our Lord Jesus Christ and our gathering together to Him, we ask you, not to be soon shaken in mind or troubled, either by spirit or by word or by letter, as if from us, as though the day of Christ had come. Let no one deceive you by any means; *for that Day will not come unless the falling away comes first,* and the man of sin is revealed, the son of perdition" (2 Thessalonians 2:1–3, emphasis added).

Apostasy will continue to increase until the day of God's judgment. In His Olivet Discourse, Jesus said, "And because lawlessness will abound, the love of many will grow cold" (Matthew 24:12). Let's focus on three specific reasons this can happen.

Some Fall Away Because They Are Deceived

There are many deceivers in our day, but the most dangerous are the ones who operate in the spiritual realm. Look at this passage: "Now the Spirit expressly says that in latter times some will depart from the faith, giving heed to deceiving spirits and doctrines of demons, speaking lies in hypocrisy, having their own conscience seared with a hot iron" (1 Timothy 4:1–2). This passage goes on to warn of false teachers who traffic in lies and hypocrisy. These men and women attempt to cause spiritual damage for their own benefit, without moral sensitivity or spiritual compasses. Such people are operating within the Church today, and their drive to deceive will continue escalating with each passing year.

Some Fall Away Because They Are Disillusioned

Tragically, others fall away because of disillusionment and perceived disappointment. Jesus explained this in His parable about seeds, which illustrated the reasons people fall away from the gospel. The seeds represented the gospel message. He said: "Those by the wayside are the ones who hear; then the devil comes and takes away the word out of their hearts, lest they should believe and be saved. But the ones on the rock are those who, when they hear, receive the word with joy; and these have no root, who believe for a while and in time of temptation fall away. Now the ones that fell among thorns are those who, when they have heard, go out and are choked with cares, riches, and pleasures of life, and bring no fruit to maturity" (Luke 8:12–14). Notice, the first reason people reject the gospel is that "the devil comes and takes away the word out of their hearts." That's deception—the deceiving spirits and demons we mentioned above.

The second reason is more complicated. Jesus described those who hear the good news and "receive the word with joy." These people are genuinely excited about Christianity. They've seen the brokenness of the world, and they've felt the brokenness in their own spirits. They know there must be something better. These people encounter the truth and receive the message with joy and hopefulness. But stony-ground believers "have no root." In times of temptation, they fall away. Many of these people are looking for a solution rather than a Savior. Sooner or later, they fall away. There's a lot in the world to cause disappointment and disillusion, and if we aren't firmly rooted in Christ and in His Word, it creates spiritual danger for us.

It's been relatively easy to live as a Christian in America throughout recent decades. However, the days seem to be coming when lifting up the banner of Christ will cost something. Christians with little or no roots in the gospel will decide the cost is too great, and they will turn their backs on Christ.

Some Fall Away Because They Are Distracted

Jesus's third explanation for the parable of the sower points to another reason apostasy has been prevalent throughout history: "Now the ones that fell among thorns are those who, when they have heard, go out and are choked with cares, riches, and pleasures of life, and bring no fruit to maturity" (Luke 8:14). The pull of desire is too strong, and they let go of their faith in order to grab all the world offers with both hands.

Remember Judas the disciple? He was among Jesus's inner circle. Yet Judas still fell away. He betrayed Christ. Judas allowed himself to be distracted by goals or desires that were based on self rather than serving the Lord. He was the treasurer of the apostolic band and kept their joint purse. He also fell into terrible sin over thirty pieces of silver. The same can happen to apparent followers of Jesus today. God has chosen us to be here as His witnesses at this critical time in history. We cannot afford to become so tangled up with the cares of life and with riches that the Word of God is choked in our lives. So, as Francis Shaeffer asked, "How should we then live?"

Where Do We Go From Here?

Let's discuss what we can do in light of all this. It's easy to become discouraged when we consider the prevalence of apostasy in the Church and in our world. Like Jonah in the Old Testament, all of us will face the choice between giving up and moving forward in our spiritual lives. This is the choice between comfort and the cross—between living for ourselves and living as servants of Christ.

Examine Yourselves

The apostle Paul was concerned about the troubled church in Corinth. Some of these believers weren't displaying much transformation in their lives. Some had lapsed into sexual sin. There was division in the church.

They argued about theological matters. And some were partaking of the Lord's Supper in a thoughtless manner. Because Paul believed many of the Corinthians were truly saved, he gave them further admonitions and instructions. But when he got to the end of his second letter, he added these important words in 2 Corinthians 13:5: "Examine yourselves to see whether you are in the faith; test yourselves. Do you not realize that Christ Jesus is in you—unless, of course, you fail the test?" (NIV).

The most important thing you can do in response to this lesson is to make sure that you are a Christian. And you are not a Christian just because you grew up in a church. You are not a Christian just because your parents are Christians. You are not a Christian because you have lived a good life. And you are not a Christian because you have served in a church and done great things for God.

One of the most sobering passages in the Bible is found in Matthew 7, where Jesus said: "Not everyone who says to Me 'Lord, Lord,' shall enter the kingdom of heaven, but he who does the will of My Father in heaven. Many will say to Me in that day, 'Lord, Lord, have we not prophesied in Your name, cast out demons in Your name, and done many wonders in Your name?' And then I will declare to them, 'I never knew you; depart from Me, you who practice lawlessness!'" (verses 21–23)

Now, remember the balance. On the one hand, we don't want to have a false assurance of salvation. But on the other hand, we do want a firm assurance that we're saved. God will help us find that balance if we'll ask Him. The psalmist taught us to pray, "Search me, O God, and know my heart; try me, and know my anxieties; and see if there is any wicked way in me, and lead me in the way everlasting" (Psalm 139:23–24).

Encourage Yourselves

That leads me to the second bit of advice. Encourage yourself in the Lord. We learn this technique from David, who came to a very disheartening moment in his life. First Samuel 30:6 says: "But David encouraged himself in the LORD his God" (KJV).

If we learn to do this, we will never fall away—and the devil can't push us around. We learn to encourage ourselves in the Lord. When we listen to the devil, we're led in the wrong direction. When we listen to friends, we get mixed advice. When we listen to our doubts, fears, worries, and feelings, we grow confused. Sometimes there's no one to preach to us, so we must say, like the psalmist, "Why are you cast down, O my soul? And why are you disquieted within me? Hope in God" (Psalm 42:11).

Sometimes we try too hard to squeeze encouragement from someone else. There are some needs only God can meet. It's unfair to expect our husband or wife or pastor or friend to do for us what only the Lord Himself can do. Instead of succumbing to discouragement and despair, we can strengthen ourselves in the Lord.

When our faith is faltering, that is when we need to turn to God. There may not be anyone else around in whom you can place your trust, but you can trust God. So, place your faith in Him and encourage yourself in your faith and strengthen yourself in your faith. You will notice that all of these passages use the word "yourself" or "himself." You must not wait for someone else to do this for you. This is your responsibility.

Exercise Yourselves

The Bible says, "For bodily exercise profits a little, but godliness is profitable for all things, having promise of the life that now is and of that which is to come" (1 Timothy 4:8). Being diligent in the care of the soul is important when it comes to resisting the temptation to fall away. Hebrews 11:6 says that God is "a rewarder of those who diligently seek Him."

The apostle Peter said, "Therefore, brethren, be even more diligent to make your call and election sure, for if you do these things you will never stumble" (2 Peter 1:10).

"These things" refers back to eight character qualities listed in verses 5-7: faith, virtue, knowledge, self-control, perseverance, godliness, brotherly kindness, and love. Could Peter have been more emphatic? If we keep growing in these traits, we'll never stumble.

Now, let me make one thing clear. When Peter says we will never stumble, he doesn't mean we will never make a mistake or commit a sin. He means we'll never shipwreck our faith. We'll never fall away from Christ. That becomes clear in The New Living Translation: "So, dear brothers and sisters, work hard to prove that you really are among those God has called and chosen. Do these things, and you will never fall away."

Well, there we have it, don't we? If we examine ourselves, encourage ourselves, and exercise ourselves in godliness and godly habits, we will never fall away.

The book of Jude is a small one-page letter near the end of the Bible. It's all about the dangers of false teachers and the temptation to fall away. Reading Jude can help us make the right choices when facing pressure. His words are critical for those of us living in a culture and in a Church defined by increasing apostasy.

Jude wrote to Christians experiencing double pressure. They faced extreme persecution, and they were under spiritual attack from heresies of all kinds. Most of the influential leaders of the Early Church had been martyred—including Peter, Paul, and James—which left both churches and individual Christians feeling vulnerable.

In the darkness of that moment, Jude's epistle provided a ray of hope. In just two verses near the end of his tiny epistle, Jude explained to Christians how to remain committed to Christ during a time of increased apostasy: "But you, beloved, building yourselves up on your most holy faith . . . . keep yourselves in the love of God" (verses 20–21).

Jude was speaking to Christians, and the phrase "building yourselves up" conveys the idea of continuation. Jude was not speaking of a one-time event but rather a life-long process. In other words, Jude told us to keep building ourselves up.

The key to withstanding apostasy is for each of us to intentionally keep taking steps to build our faith through learning, growing, seeking out God's will, and obeying everything He commands us to do.

We must continue to cultivate our relationship with the Lord. Our walk with God is not static. We are either growing in Him or we are beginning to grow cold toward Him. This is why God warned the church in Ephesus, "Nevertheless I have this against you, that you have left your first love. Remember therefore from where you have fallen; repent and do the first works" (Revelation 2:4–5).

Examine yourself, encourage yourself, and exercise yourself in the Lord. And most of all just keep going and growing. Don't stop! Don't look back! Just keep walking with the Lord.

Now to Him who is able to keep you from stumbling,
And to present you faultless
Before the presence of His glory with exceeding joy,
To God our Savior,
Who alone is wise,
Be glory and majesty,
Dominion and power,
Both now and forever.
Amen (Jude 24–25).

APPLICATION

Personal Questions

1. Read Hebrews 2:1–4. Pay careful attention to the references to the "falling away" we have studied in this chapter.

   a. What does the author of Hebrews say will keep us from "drifting away" (verse 1)?

   b. How does this portion of Scripture remind you of what is ahead for those who "neglect so great salvation" (verses 2 and 3)?

   c. How can you be careful to avoid falling away from your faith based on this passage?

2. Read Matthew 24:3–14. Reread the verses in the Olivet Discourse directly dealing with the falling away of believers from their faith.

   a. What are three of the signs Jesus says will be the beginning of birth pains?

   b. How does Jesus say many people will be led to fall away (verses 4–5)?

   c. What is one weakness of yours that might tempt you to fall away from your faith?

3. Read John 6:66–71.

   a. Briefly scan John 6 and try to determine what caused so many of the Lord's crowds to fall away.

   b. What do you think of Peter's logic (verses 68–69)? Analyze his answer in the space below.

c. Nevertheless, Jesus predicted another tragic defection. If you were directing a movie of this scene, how would you expect Jesus to deliver those lines? Can you see His heart and mood through His words?

Group Questions

1. Read the book of Jude as a group. Think especially about how this book relates to your group as you read.

    a. Jude tells us to build ourselves up in what two ways (verse 20)?

    b. How can we as the Church do a better job of building each other up?

    c. What is the key to not falling away (verse 21)?

    d. What does "looking for the mercy of our Lord Jesus Christ" look like lived out in our lives?

e. In what practical ways are you going to keep each other from falling away this week?

f. How does Jude describe those whom Jesus protects from stumbling (verse 24)?

g. How does this description change our relationships, interactions, attitudes, actions, and ultimately every aspect of our lives?

2. Read Hebrews 12:1–2.

a. What does the author of Hebrews mean by "so great a cloud of witnesses" (verse 1)?

b. How does this "cloud of witnesses" reference apply to your group?

c. How can you "run with endurance the race that is set before us" in your walk with the Lord this week (verse 1)?

d. How does the author of Hebrews encourage his readers to gain the strength to run with this endurance (verse 2)?

DID YOU KNOW?

Jude, one of the shortest books in the Bible, was written by Jesus's half-brother and James's brother. Although he is not often referenced in the Gospels, he was one of the twelve apostles. He was a first-century missionary and one of the most influential Early Church leaders. Interestingly, although this claim has not been fully verified, it is also reported that Jude was a vegetarian. Jude has been depicted from time to time holding an ax, ironically the reported weapon of his martyrdom in Syria. As a slight to Jude, the Roman Catholic Church made him the patron saint of lost causes due to his relative anonymity.

A BIOGRAPHICAL PROPHECY— END TIMES PEOPLE

2 TIMOTHY 3:13

In this lesson we learn about the increasing evil that will characterize many people in the Last Days and how to counter their influence.

The world is full of people whose sinful behavior is going from bad to worse. This has been the case since the fall of humanity in Genesis 3; but things seem to be getting worse, as the Bible predicted. The Lord has given us many prophecies about the Last Days, with warnings they will be perilous. Even as society becomes more godless, we can counter its influence through the light of Christ in our lives.

OUTLINE

I. What Does This Mean?
    A. Selfish People
    B. Splintered Families
    C. Shattered Societies

II. Where Do We Go From Here?
- A. Remember the Grace You Received
- B. Reflect the Light You Have Become
- C. Reveal the Darkness You See

OVERVIEW

Why do good people go the wrong way and do bad things? The Bible's answer is sin. It's the fundamental problem of every person. Romans 3:10–12 says, "No one is righteous—not even one. No one is truly wise; no one is seeking God. . . . No one does good, not a single one" (NLT). Our problem is that we live in a world of sinful people. Sin is lust and murder, but sin is also impatience and self-absorption. Our sin affects everything.

Sin is a blood disease that entered our bloodstream through Adam and Eve when they rebelled against God in His garden, and this disease has descended through the generations to the present. The Bible says, "Therefore, just as through one man sin entered the world, and death through sin, and thus death spread to all men, because all sinned" (Romans 5:12). The prophet Jeremiah wrote, "The heart is deceitful above all things, and desperately wicked; who can know it?" (17:9) Because of this, Jesus said, "For without Me you can do nothing" (John 15:5). The blood of Christ and the Spirit of God must unleash their power in our lives if we're to be godly people.

But there's a troubling trend in today's world. Rampant godlessness is overtaking our culture. Things have reached a tipping point. Gun violence. Depression. Obesity. Homicide. Addiction. Choose the negative headline, and chances are it has been increasing dramatically over the past decade. Something is broken in us, and we've nearly given up the fight against it.

What Does This Mean?

The apostle Paul wrote his final letter to Timothy, his son in the faith, from a Roman cell. Near the end of his letter, Paul drew a surprisingly detailed picture of how people will behave prior to the Tribulation. "But know this," he wrote, "that in the last days perilous times will come: For men will be lovers of themselves, lovers of money, boasters, proud, blasphemers, disobedient to parents, unthankful, unholy, unloving, unforgiving, slanderers, without self-control, brutal, despisers of good, traitors, headstrong, haughty, lovers of pleasure rather than lovers of God, having a form of godliness but denying its power" (2 Timothy 3:1–5). He added in verse 13: "But evil men and impostors will grow worse and worse, deceiving and being deceived."

"Worse and worse!" With those three short words, Paul predicted people will descend into rampant and accelerating godlessness as we approach the Tribulation. Please note the apostle's focus is not on bad times but on bad people. As John Calvin wrote, "The hardness or danger of this time is in Paul's view to be, not war, famine or diseases, nor any of the other calamities or ills that befall the body, but the wicked and depraved ways of men."[1]

Paul gave us nineteen specific character descriptions of what people will be like. In other words, here in 2 Timothy 3, the Lord gives us nineteen expressions to depict the nature of godlessness in the Last Days. We can't bore into all nineteen words and phrases in this study, but we can see a pattern in them. Paul's words move from selfish people to splintered families to shattered societies.

Selfish People

Right up front, the Lord tells us that the Last Days will be populated by people who are lovers of themselves (verse 2). The origin of our modern word *narcissism* is the excessive love of self. According to Paul, the days before the Tribulation will be perilous because people will love only themselves. They will accordingly be "boasters, proud, blasphemers" (verse 2). These people love to talk about themselves and to build themselves up. Such people want everyone else to love them as much as they love themselves. They write their own press reports and pad their own resumes. When you finally meet the person in question, you hardly recognize them. These are proud or haughty people, which means they're disdainful toward others. Looking down on others comes as naturally to them as it does to a pigeon atop a statue.

The word *blasphemer* is a theological term referring to verbal abuse toward God. The original Greek word also included the idea of slander. Those who harbor a disproportionate love for themselves, being boastful of themselves and disdainful of others, expend a lot of energy seeking to reduce everyone around them. They're intent on pushing others aside so they can stand taller. Selfish people pull others down; it's in their nature.

Splintered Families

The increasing sinfulness of the Last Days will manifest itself in selfish people, and those selfish people will unavoidably create damaged families. The days prior to the Tribulation will be strewn with broken homes.

There are five descriptive terms in 2 Timothy 3 that highlight the damage broken people will perpetrate on their own families in the Last Days. People will be disobedient to parents, unthankful, unholy, unloving, and unforgiving.

Children will be *disobedient*. Willfully, they will do what they want to do, casting off oversight and authority. They will ignore the instruction of Scripture that says, "Children, obey your parents in the Lord, for this is right" (Ephesians 6:1).

They will be *ungrateful*. Gone will be a thankful spirit between children and their parents, and that lack of gratitude will extend to other relationships as well.

The third word is *unholy*. In this context, that implies lack of respect. There will be no respect within the structure or framework of the family; people will reject authority and harbor a growing sense of rebellion and independence.

Next, we come to the word *unloving*. Normal human affection will wither away. Homes will become hard places ruined by harsh hearts, which will spill over into the whole society.

The final word is *unforgiving*, which could also be translated as "truth breaker." Rebellious people's stubbornness and hardheartedness will grow into an emotional forest of poisonous trees bearing toxic fruit. They will lack the capacity to forgive others, which paradoxically means they'll live as though they themselves could never be forgiven for all the harm they've caused.

How should God's people live in the midst of it all? It's very simple. In Christ, it's not appropriate to negate virtue. Our homes should be filled with obedience between children and parents. Families should be filled with gratitude and defined by respect. They should exude a natural love and affection. And we should be able to trust each other. We must be doggedly committed to biblical marriages and to kingdom families. Whatever has happened in the past, our homes must be indwelled by Jesus Christ.

Shattered Societies

Dr. Tony Evans recently spoke about the ripple effect of sin on society: "If you're a messed-up man and you have a family, you're going to help make a messed-up family. If you are a messed-up man contributing to a messed-up family, and your messed-up family goes to church, then your messed-up family's gonna make its contribution to a messed-up church. . . . If you're a messed-up man contributing to a messed-up family resulting in a messed-up church causing a messed-up neighborhood, and your neighborhood's part of a city, well, your messed-up neighborhood's gonna make its contribution to a messed-up city. . . . If you're a messed-up man contributing to a messed-up family resulting in a messed-up church causing a messed-up neighborhood that resides in a messed-up city that's part of a messed-up county, and your county's part of the state, well, now, your messed-up county's gonna make its contribution to a messed-up state. . . .

"If you're a messed-up man contributing to a messed-up family resulting in a messed-up church causing a messed-up neighborhood that resides in a messed-up city that's part of a messed-up county contributing to a messed-up state, and your state's part of the country, well, now, your messed-up state's gonna make its contribution to a messed-up nation. If you're a messed-up man contributing to a messed-up family resulting in a messed-up church causing a messed-up neighborhood that resides in a messed-up city that's part of a messed-up county that's contributing to a messed-up state that's contributing to a messed-up country, and your country's part of the world, well, now, your messed-up country is gonna make its contribution to a messed-up world."[2]

Dr. Evans is describing the same progression as the apostle Paul in 2 Timothy 3:1–5. Paul began by describing the selfishness of end times people. That selfishness will contribute to the decline of end times families. And the more broken families you find within a society, the more broken that society will become. That's what we see in the final section of those nineteen descriptors. The culture of the Last Days will be dominated by "slanderers, without self-control, brutal, despisers of good, traitors, headstrong, haughty, lovers of pleasure rather than lovers of God, having a form of godliness but denying its power" (verses 3–5).

Where Do We Go From Here?

How do Christians live in such a place—in this world where selfishness reigns and immorality increases? How can we be a different kind of "End Times people" in a dark world?

Benjamin Franklin described the darkness that filled the streets of Philadelphia in his day, causing an increase in crime and an overall lack of safety. He was unsuccessful in convincing the city to light their porches, but he still put up one light pole in front of his own house. The lamp cast light on the street, giving passersby a feeling of well-being and safety. Pretty soon, almost the whole city was lighting the walkways in front of their houses at night. Our example is often greater than our admonitions and campaigns.

With that in mind, let's move from 2 Timothy 3 and look at Ephesians 5. This is the passage that says: "For you were once darkness, but now you are light in the Lord." That sentence—Ephesians 5:8—is short enough to memorize, but powerful enough to illuminate the pathways around our lives.

Remember the Grace You Received

How do we walk in the light when our society is defined by End Times people? First, by experiencing God's grace through an encounter with the Lord Jesus Christ. Metaphors involving light pervade Scripture, and Ephesians 5:8 describes the difference that comes over us when we have a grace experience with Christ. There is a moment when the full grace of God, manifested physically when He sent Christ to this earth to be crucified and wash us clean of our sin, enter our lives, and change us from the inside out. Before that moment, we live in darkness. We are spiritually, morally, personally, and eternally in pitch blackness.

But this darkness does not have to overcome us. The moment we come to Christ, He pushes down the lever that connects us to the throne of grace and switches on His light inside us. Many Christians describe their moment of grace in bright terms. We read story after story of people who were dead in the darkness of their sin, but they come alive when God's light illuminates their lives, expels the darkness of their sin, and leaves them forever changed. They begin to glow with the light of Christ, eager to share their transformation so others might be transformed by the light of Christ. The same happens inside each of us the more we remember the grace we have received.

Reflect the Light You Have Become

Next, we must exude God's light. That's what we read in Ephesians 5:8–10: "Walk as children of light (for the fruit of the Spirit is in all goodness, righteousness, and truth), finding out what is acceptable to the Lord." Too many Christians are trying to achieve a sort of grayness without being different and distinct from the world. But we must walk and live as children of light.

Psalm 34:5 says, "They looked to Him and were radiant, and their faces were not ashamed." Isaiah 60:5 says, "Then you shall see and become radiant, and your heart shall swell with joy." What exactly does that mean? Paul tells us plainly in his parenthetical statement in verse 9. Those who are radiant and who walk in the light demonstrate the fruit of the Spirit in all goodness, righteousness, and truth.

People of goodness. In our relationships, we walk toward Christ and share the essential goodness of Christ through His Spirit working within us. This goodness is a characteristic of those who have been delivered from the darkness and are now walking in the light. Elsewhere in the Bible, we see it stated like this: "See that no one renders evil for evil to anyone, but always pursue what is good both for yourselves and for all" (1 Thessalonians 5:15).

Before God transformed us, we were pursuing evil as fast as we could. But now we've become Christians, which prompts us to look for ways to do good works. We are pursuing good for ourselves and for all people. It's a quality we can never outlive.

People of righteousness. Our relationship to God is one of righteousness. Paul told Timothy, "But you, man of God, flee from all this, and pursue righteousness" (1 Timothy 6:11, NIV). *Pursue* means "to chase after" and "to hunt down." We are pursuing, trying to chase down, running hard after righteousness. In these perilous days, we need this action in all our habits— and a righteous God in our daily experience.

People of truth. Walking in the light also makes us people of truth, men and women of integrity. Our outward persona must be matched by inward reality. We want to bring God's truth into every situation, bearing Christ's truth with kindness and love.

As Christians, we must live out the words of Christ: "You are the light of the world. A city that is set on a hill cannot be hidden" (Matthew 5:14). We must always "proclaim the praises of Him who called [us] out of darkness into His marvelous light" (1 Peter 2:9).

Reveal the Darkness You See

Ephesians continues like this: "And have no fellowship with the unfruitful works of darkness, but rather expose them.... All things that are exposed are made manifest by the light, for whatever makes manifest is light. Therefore He says: 'Awake, you who sleep, arise from the dead, and Christ will give you light'" (Ephesians 5:11–14). Christ changes our relationships. Some people will turn away from us, but some of them will follow our trail of light and find Christ for themselves.

In Christ's light, we can no longer participate in fellowship with those who are doing the works of darkness. That doesn't mean we reject these people or stop loving them, but we can no longer participate with them in ungodly things. We are still *in* the world, but we're no longer *of* the world. As Jesus warned us, "Everyone practicing evil hates the light and does not come to the light, lest his deeds should be exposed. But he who does the truth comes to the light" (John 3:20–21).

When Almighty God comes into our lives, He changes us. He gives us a new description—being children of light. He gives us a new direction—walking toward His light. We have a new desire—pursuing the will of God. We have a new distinction—no longer walking according to the unfruitful works of darkness. And we have a new duty—spreading His light. When Jesus Christ comes into your life, He switches on the light that can never be turned off!

In Ephesians 1:7–8, Paul writes that in Christ "we have redemption through His blood, the forgiveness of sins, according to the riches of His grace, which He made to abound toward us in all wisdom." The gospel of grace, which says that each of us matters and has worth as God's image bearers, redeems us. It says we are not defined by our failures and our faults but by a love without merit or condition.

We're living in a messed-up world filled with self-centered, self-absorbed, self-indulgent people. The Bible warns that in the Last Days perilous times will come. Society will go from bad to worse. But remember, the city of Ephesus was also a place of darkness in Paul's day. Yet he viewed the Christians there as children of light. Their presence lit up the city streets with the glow of Jesus.

Even in dark days, we can experience God's grace, exude His radiance, and exhibit His holiness. So, let's brighten up! In a world increasingly dominated by End Times people, He has empowered us to shine.

APPLICATION

Personal Questions

1. Read 2 Timothy 3:1–9.

   a. What kind of people does Paul describe? In what ways do they fail to uphold God's standards for their lives as given in Scripture?

   b. What is it about these people that is different from a faithful Christian?

   c. How can you be careful to avoid the attributes that Paul ascribes to these people?

   d. How does Paul tell us to deal with these people (verse 5)?

   e. What does verse 7 say about these people? How is that important for you as you pursue Christ and seek to be His light in the world around you?

   f. What encouragement does Paul give in verse 9? How should that change your attitude as you deal with these people?

2. Read Ephesians 1:7–8.

   a. What do these verses say about God's grace?

   b. Why is that relevant to you as you seek to live out His commands in your life?

   c. How is God's grace related to the blood of Jesus Christ? What does verse 7 say about Jesus' blood?

3. How can you share these truths with others this week? What is one practical way to live out God's light and grace this week?

Group Questions

1. Read Ephesians 5:8–14.

   a. What does verse 8 say about our transformation?

   b. How often do we fail to live this way, and what can we do to improve that?

   c. Where is the fruit of the light found (verse 9)?

   d. How can we live out the command in verse 10? In what ways can we encourage one another to do that this week?

   e. What does verse 11 say our light should shine on? How can we do this and still be loving?

   f. What examples have you seen of people failing to radiate Christ's light in this world, either by not loving enough or not holding to His truth enough? Discuss.

g. How can you make sure as a group not to do this in your own walk with
the Lord?

h. How does Paul describe the multiplication effect of God's light shining
on us and illuminating others around us (verse 13)?

i. What is one area of your life that needs the transforming light of Christ
to shine on it?

j. What promise does Paul give in verse 14? How can that help us as we
seek to live for Christ this week?

k. What do people who live out God's light look like? How can we follow
their example?

DID YOU KNOW?

When people talk about lightspeed, they are referencing the incredible 671 million miles per hour at which light travels. Traveling at a typical highway speed limit would get you to the sun in 157 years, but light only takes 8 minutes and 20 seconds to reach the sun. How powerful is the light used as a metaphor for the influence of Christ! And not only that, but the sun upholds our entire life on earth. Without it, there would be no weather patterns, plants, oxygen, or food. It is critical to every aspect of our lives, just like Jesus.

Notes
1. John Calvin, *The Second Epistle of Paul the Apostle to the Corinthians and the Epistles to Timothy, Titus, and Philemon* (Grand Rapids, MI: Eerdmans, 1996), 322.
2. Tony Evans, "Why Men Matter," *Sermons.Love,* https://sermons.love//tony-evans/4411-tony-evans-why-men-matter.html.

LESSON 7

A POLITICAL PROPHECY— CANCEL CULTURE

MATTHEW 24:10–12

In this lesson we learn about the dangers of the current cancel culture and how to counter it with the love of Christ.

The gospel of Christ is one of love and forgiveness. Jesus gave people second chances, and He corrected them in love. But the cancel culture of today is the exact opposite, seeking to censor differing opinions and sometimes even ruin careers in the interest of keeping people in line with the views of social media and political pundits. There are few things less loving than publicly excoriating random people. Yet that's what cancel culture demands.

OUTLINE

I. What Does This Mean?
A. A Culture of Disdain

B. A Culture of Deception

C. A Culture of Disconnection

II. Where Do We Go From Here?
A. It Takes Wisdom
B. It Takes Courage
C. It Takes Forgiveness
D. It Takes Love

OVERVIEW

The word *cancel* once described what we did to subscriptions or faltering television programs. In today's society, canceling someone is a punishment for violating a set of unwritten rules currently in play throughout much of the liberal world.

First, there's an attempt to publicly humiliate the person by flagrantly exposing the supposed wrong he or she committed. Second, he or she is pushed mercilessly to confess and apologize. Simply to be accused means a retraction, and an apology is expected. And third, attempts are made to remove that person from public conversation. As a result, people are fired, mocked, threatened, de-platformed, and delegitimized in every way.

This approach to culture is unbiblical, and yet it's the direction our society has taken. Jesus commanded: "'You shall love the Lord your God with all your heart, with all your soul, and with all your mind.' This is the first and greatest commandment. And the second is like it: 'You shall love your neighbor as yourself'" (Matthew 22:37–39).

Jesus spent time with canceled people. Jesus approached the woman at the well and offered her the water of life. He had fellowship with lepers and sinners and blessed children when others tried to nudge them away. He expressed compassion for a woman taken in adultery and comforted a murderer nailed to a cross beside Him. Jesus had no place in His heart for the cancel culture, but He was wonderful at demonstrating God's love and grace to everyone. He still is.

What Does This Mean?

Society is becoming more intolerant and polarized by the day, and we may not see a reversal of these trends. The more insidious elements of cancel culture are a malignant form of the spitefulness and self-importance common to all human nature. What we're seeing today reminds us of what Jesus described in Matthew 24, which was our Lord's sermon about the Last Days and the Great Tribulation.

Jesus warned of a coming period of world distress, saying: "For then there will be great tribulation, such as has not been since the beginning of the world until this time, no, nor ever shall be. And unless those days were shortened, no flesh would be saved; but for the elect's sake those days will be shortened" (Matthew 24:21–22).

Leading up to this Great Tribulation, Jesus predicted a series of signs that will foreshadow the end of history. He spoke of wars and rumors of wars, famines, earthquakes, and pestilences. Then He said: "These are the beginning of sorrows. . . . And then many will be offended, will betray one another, and will hate one another. Then many false prophets will rise up and deceive many. And because lawlessness will abound, the love of many will grow cold" (Matthew 24:8–12). There are several terms in those two verses that represent the ethos of cancel culture.

A Culture of Disdain

First, Jesus talked about how easily people would be offended in the days leading up to the Tribulation. He linked being easily offended with hating one another and betraying one another. The Greek word translated "betray" is important. It doesn't mean betrayal in the sense of saying negative things about coworkers in order to get a promotion instead of them. Nor does it mean betrayal in terms of deceiving others or turning on someone who used to be a friend—stabbing them in the back. Instead, the text is talking about betrayal in the sense of intentionally revealing or exposing something that is hidden.

In other words, Jesus said society leading up to the End Times would be marked by people who actively root up, expose, and betray those around them. This betrayal is commonplace in our world today, and it makes up an essential ingredient of the toxic stew we call cancel culture.

In many ways, cancel culture is dependent on betrayal. We all have mistakes in our past we'd like to forget. But in a world fueled by cancel culture, those mistakes are not allowed to remain in the past. People intentionally dig through the histories and biographies and social media posts of others—even those they consider friends—in order to drag those mistakes into the present. The vitriol we see on social media today is evidence of something new. Our children need to be taught not to destroy one another, though they are surrounded by a culture that glorifies hatred, abuse, and exploitation. We're living in a culture of disdain.

A Culture of Deception

In His great sermon on the End Times, Jesus also warned of the rise of many false prophets who would deceive multitudes (Matthew 24:11). That's never been easier than today due to social media. Most at risk are senior citizens, who lost about a billion dollars in 2020 due to online scams. Fake people, fake reviews, fake products, fake news, fake friends—all of this has come to us via the world of Big Tech. And all of this is contributing to a growing culture of deception.

A Culture of Disconnection

The next logical step? Disconnection. In a culture marked by disdain and deception, people want to withdraw from society in any way possible. Jesus put it like this: "And because lawlessness will abound, the love of many will grow cold" (Matthew 24:12).

Apologist Abdu Murray had this to say about the relationally frightening nature of today's society: "In cancel culture, a single mistake is perpetually unforgivable because it's not simply a guilty act. Rather, the mistake defines the individual's identity, turning them into a shameful person—someone who can be 'canceled.'"[1]

The culture leading up to the Tribulation and the end of history will be characterized by coldness in our feelings for one another and in our dealings with each other. It will be marked by isolation and disconnection. Shame will drive people inward. Bullying will drive them downward. Hatred will drive them backward.

We all know about physical pain and emotional pain, but our society is suffering from social pain. According to *Healthline*, "Social pain involves painful emotions caused by situations involving other people, such as feeling rejected, alone, ostracized, devalued, abandoned, or disconnected."[2]

The root cause of disconnection is spiritual in nature. When we are disconnected from God, we don't have love, joy, peace, patience, or kindness to show to others. We become isolated in our self-centeredness.

We see these realities at play in the cancel culture of our modern world. It's not difficult to understand why such a society would lead to relational indifference and isolation. After all, relationships become risky. A good relationship requires us to be vulnerable, but why choose to be vulnerable to other people when they could use our faults to cancel us?

We're witnessing the consequences of this disconnection firsthand. As hatred and deception have increased, love in our world has decreased. Our relationships have gone cold.

Where Do We Go From Here?

Now that we understand more about cancel culture and the dangers it poses, where can we go from here? What does it take to live in such a world? Here's an even greater question: What does it take to live for Christ? What does it take to create a different kind of culture at home? At work? At church?

The short answer is—a lot! It's not easy to live as members of God's kingdom in a world that's increasingly hostile to His values. This is the shared experience of every generation of Christians since the first one, so we've had two thousand years to prepare for these days. One thing we know: The rewards of following Christ are worth it. So, let's explore four uncancellable concepts.

It Takes Wisdom

Jesus told us, "Behold, I send you out as sheep in the midst of wolves. Therefore be wise as serpents and harmless as doves" (Matthew 10:16).

Wisdom is a word that confuses people today. True wisdom is the ability to discern what is right, good, just, and proper. Wisdom also shares true information with others as temperately as possible. Doesn't it make us cringe when we see Christians losing their tempers while trying to share truths? We can't avoid the culture wars, but the tone of our conversation is critical.

Colossians 4:6 says, "Let your conversation be gracious as well as sensible, for then you will have the right answer for everyone" (TLB).

We don't need to pick fights with those who disagree with us. On the other hand, we don't need to stay silent when our faith is challenged. As Solomon said, "Even a fool is counted wise when he holds his peace; when he shuts his lips, he is considered perceptive" (Proverbs 17:28).

There are also moments when followers of Jesus need to stand firmly for the truth. And when those moments come, we must speak and write and teach with the same boldness Stephen demonstrated before his accusers in the Sanhedrin. May it be said of us, as it was said of him, that those who hear our words will be "cut to the heart" (Acts 7:54). Knowing what to say, when to say it, and how to say it—that is wisdom. And that's what we need!

The book of James contrasts the wisdom from below and the wisdom from above. The wisdom from below is "earthly, sensual, demonic. For where envy and self-seeking exist, confusion and every evil thing are there. But the wisdom that is from above is first pure, then peaceable, gentle, willing to yield, full of mercy and good fruits, without partiality and without hypocrisy" (James 3:15–17).

Notice that James contrasted worldly wisdom with sensuality, demonic thinking, envy, self-seeking egos, confusion, and every evil thing. Those are the fruits of cancel culture. But true wisdom is from above. It is a gift from God, available to all in the humility of Jesus Christ. James said, "If any of you lacks wisdom, let him ask of God, who gives to all liberally and without reproach, and it will be given to him" (James 1:5).

That is the challenge for Christians as we seek to navigate the troubled waters of cancel culture. Ask God for His wisdom. Ask in faith, believing the truth of His Word. Pray for discernment, and He will provide it.

It Takes Courage

The Bible says, "Be strong and of good courage, do not fear nor be afraid of them; for the LORD your God, He is the One who goes with you. He will not leave you nor forsake you" (Deuteronomy 31:6). We need to heed those commands if we want to live meaningfully as followers of Jesus in a world influenced by cancel culture. We need courage because there will be times when staying close to Christ means taking a stand. And that stand will likely come at a cost.

John Piper offers this reminder: "Christian courage is the willingness to say and do the right thing regardless of the earthly cost, because God promises to help you and save you on account of Christ. An act takes courage, and it will likely be painful. The pain may be physical, as in war and rescue operations. Or the pain may be mental as in confrontation and controversy." Either way, according to Piper, "Courage is indispensable for both spreading and preserving the truth of Christ."[3]

The word *bold* occurs repeatedly in the book of Acts to describe the attitude of the early Christians who were infused with courage by the Holy Spirit. For example, Acts 4:31 says, "And when they had prayed, the place where they were assembled together was shaken; and they were all filled with the Holy Spirit, and they spoke the word of God with boldness."

Kindness and courage—those two God-given personality traits are crucial in critical times. We see these qualities in the life of the Old Testament prophet Jeremiah. He remained committed to God and to his prophetic work even in the midst of extreme criticism. Jeremiah was faithful to his ministry even when those attacks came from his own people. He declared the words of the Lord during a particularly difficult period of Israel's history, and he didn't falter as things grew worse around him.

His hearers tried to cancel him. They said, "Come and let us devise plans against Jeremiah; for the law shall not perish from the priest, nor counsel from the wise, nor the word from the prophet. Come and let us attack him with the tongue, and let us not give heed to any of his words" (Jeremiah 18:18). Yet Jeremiah persisted in his ministry. He continued to speak the truth as a representative of Almighty God.

The mob will mock and malign us. Society will shame and slander us. Associates will assault and attack us. The crowds may even want to kill us. Through it all, we must have courage. We must choose to be courageous. Thankfully, that is a choice we do not make alone, nor is it a stand we take alone. God will be with us. Psalm 27:14 says, "Wait on the LORD; be of good courage, and He shall strengthen your heart." And remember—courage is contagious. Our courage will spread to others.

It Takes Forgiveness

In a world where the mistakes of the past are fair game for the present, there's no room for forgiveness or even atonement. Instead, those who are canceled are always treated as deserving of scorn, wrath, and judgment. Thankfully, the Bible offers another way.

Ephesians 4:32 says, "Be kind to one another, tenderhearted, forgiving one another, even as God in Christ forgave you." Colossians 3:12–13 adds, "Therefore, as the elect of God, holy and beloved, put on tender mercies, kindness, humility, meekness, longsuffering; bearing with one another, and forgiving one another, if anyone has a complaint against another; even as Christ forgave you, so you also must do."

When we forgive someone who has wronged us, we set them free; we also set ourselves free. Bitterness in our own hearts is like a poison that continually eats away at our joy and happiness. But when we forgive, it's liberating for both the forgiven and the forgiver.

It Takes Love

Finally, living for Jesus in a world marked by cancel culture takes love. Remember the passage in the Gospels where Jesus rescued a young woman about to be canceled? He had been teaching in the temple courts when a group of Pharisees forcibly dragged a girl in front of Him. They had caught her in the act of adultery. "Stone her!" the crowd declared. "That is the punishment proscribed by the law. She is guilty of sin, and she must be permanently removed. She is canceled."

But Jesus didn't agree. Instead of canceling that young woman, Jesus told her accusers, "He who is without sin among you, let him throw a stone at her first" (John 8:7). Then, after everyone had left in shame, Jesus spoke tenderly to the girl, saying, "Neither do I condemn you; go and sin no more" (John 8:11).

As we've seen, cancel culture is laser-focused on judgment, accusation, and punishment. The goal of those who cancel others is to broadcast their sins from pillar to post and never allow them to be removed or forgotten. Christ's goal, on the other hand, is love, mercy, and grace. In the words of Scripture, "And above all things have fervent love for one another, for 'love will cover a multitude of sins'" (1 Peter 4:8).

One day Jesus will cancel this culture itself. But for now, there is one cancel culture we should partake in. There's one cancel culture to embrace. The Bible says, "When you were dead in your sins . . . God made you alive with Christ. He forgave us all our sins, having canceled the charge of our legal indebtedness, which stood against us and condemned us; he has taken it away, nailing it to the cross" (Colossians 2:13–14, NIV).

When we come to Jesus Christ, He cancels our sins and welcomes us into His family. Instead of disdain, deception, and disconnection, He gives us love, truth, and a place by His side. He fills us with wisdom, courage, and compassion. He commissions us to meet the cancel culture with the power of the cross. We can have confidence that nothing and no one can ever cancel the One who cancels our sins.

APPLICATION

Personal Questions

1. Read Matthew 24:9–14.

    a. What does the second half of verse 9 say? How is this starting to resemble the world's attitude toward Christians today?

    b. What does verse 10 say will happen once people begin to turn away from the faith? How does that reinforce the importance of having a strengthened relationship with God in your life?

    c. How can Christians prepare for the future that is prophesied in verse 11?

d. How do you avoid being discouraged by these deceptive false prophets?

2. Read James 3:13–18.

a. What does James say is the result of wisdom lived out in one's life?

b. How is this important to you as you seek to live for Christ well?

c. Many highly ambitious people seek wisdom. How does James turn that on its head in verse 14?

d. How does James contrast earthly wisdom with heavenly wisdom in verses 15–17?

e. How can you be sure that the wisdom you seek to implement is from God and not from the world around you? What are some of the times in your life when earthly wisdom failed and heavenly wisdom was needed?

3. How does this lesson help you to better love your neighbors and reject cancel culture?

Group Questions

1. Read Colossians 3:12–13 as a group.

    a. How does Paul instruct the Colossians to clothe themselves?

    b. What would this look like lived out in our lives? How often do we fail to live like this?

    c. How does Paul instruct Christians to live among one another in verse 13?

    d. Is the Church today as a whole living up to this standard? If not, how could we do a better job of living like that?

e. How can we best forgive "as Christ forgave you"?

f. Can you think of a time when you were on the giving or receiving end of this kind of forgiveness? If comfortable, share your experience with the group.

2. Read Colossians 2:13–15 together.

a. What phrase does Paul use to describe our condition before we were saved through the blood of Christ?

b. If we kept this at the forefront of our minds, would it change the urgency we had to reach the world with the gospel of Christ? Why or why not?

c. What does verse 14 say Jesus did to whatever condemns us?

3. Based on this lesson, how can we best respond if our society tries to cancel us?

4. How can we keep a healthy perspective on God's sovereignty as we also seek to be a light in this cancel-culture-oriented world?

DID YOU KNOW?

The concept of "canceling" people has been around for close to a decade, but the concept of cancel culture has come into widespread use in the last five years. The phrase dates from 2017 and refers to a cultural boycott of someone. It largely coincided with the rise of the "Me Too" movement of 2017 and originally consisted of calling out disgraced celebrities who were accused of heinous crimes. However, it evolved beyond that, especially on social media. Today anyone can be cancelled, and an increasing number of people are finding themselves in this situation after a post or tweet goes viral and is widely condemned.

Notes
1. Abdu Murray, "Canceled: How the Eastern Honor-Shame Mentality Traveled West," *The Gospel Coalition*, May 28, 2020, https://www.thegospelcoalition.org/article/canceled-understanding-eastern-honor-shame/.
2. Cathy Cassata, "Yes, You're Probably Experiencing Social Pain Right Now: How to Cope," *Healthline*, January 25, 2021, https://www.healthline.com/health-news/yes-youre-probably-experiencing-social-pain-right-now-how-to-cope#1.-Know-your-pain-is-real.
3. John Piper, "Christian Courage," *Desiring God*, May 11, 1999, https://www.desiringgod.org/articles/christian-courage.

LESSON 8

A SPIRITUAL PROPHECY— SPIRITUAL FAMINE

AMOS 8:11

Many people who seem to start out for Christ falter along the way. In this lesson we'll discuss what's causing this and learn how to remain true and growing in the faith.

A startling number of people don't know Scripture's power. They think the Bible is a helpful guidebook, but not the Almighty God's own words. This attitude isn't limited to those without faith in Christ. Many Christians have little spiritual depth. There is a great amount of shallow Bible study and depthless sermons. We must encourage proper reverence for the Bible, along with a corresponding personal dedication to God and His Word. This will help us counter the spiritual famine stemming from a loss of appreciation of Scripture.

OUTLINE

I. What Does This Mean?
    A. Our Heritage Is Being Lost
    B. Our Theology Is Being Weakened
    C. Our Bibles Are Being Overlooked
    D. Our Appetite Is Being Ruined

II. Where Do We Go From Here?
A. Be Burdened
B. Be Students
C. Be Shepherds
D. Be Evangelistic

OVERVIEW

The Bible teaches there will be a famine of truth in the Last Days. We read this specifically in the prophecy of the rugged prophet Amos. He boldly proclaimed: "Prepare to meet your God, O Israel!" (Amos 4:12) People take offense at that message in the modern world. They did in Amos' time too. "Get out of here, you prophet!" the priests and politicians said (Amos 7:12, NLT).

In response, Amos spoke this piercing prediction: "'Behold, the days are coming,' says the Lord GOD, 'That I will send a famine on the land, not a famine of bread...but of hearing the words of the LORD'" (Amos 8:11–12). Amos was describing a deadly famine that will affect the *ears* of people in the Last Days. Ezekiel declared, "Disaster will come upon disaster, and rumor will be upon rumor. Then they will seek a vision from a prophet; but the law will perish from the priest, and counsel from the elders" (Ezekiel 7:26).

In a similar prophecy, the prophet Micah warned, "Therefore you shall have night without vision, and you shall have darkness without divination; the sun shall go down on the prophets, and the day shall be dark for them" (Micah 3:6). The apostle Paul said, "But know this, that in the last days perilous times will come: For men will be ... always learning and never able to come to the knowledge of the truth" (2 Timothy 3:1–2, 7). These warnings concern a loss of hunger for Scripture, not a lack of availability. This is a self-inflicted famine.

What Does This Mean?

What we see prophesied in the book of Amos and other passages of Scripture is spiritual starvation. It's a crisis affecting not our bodies, but our souls. To appreciate the serious nature of this coming spiritual famine, we need to dig a little deeper into its implications. What does it mean for these Last Days? What does it mean for our lives right now? Here are four ways our culture is currently under threat from spiritual malnourishment.

Our Heritage Is Being Lost

The psalmist said, "You have given me the heritage of those who fear Your name" (Psalm 61:5). It's not just our knowledge of the Bible that's being lost in today's culture. It's the entirety of our Christian history. Revisionist historians have removed every shred of wholesome biblical influence from the records of America and Europe and have filled our textbooks with the questionable contributions of everyone else. How many school children know the first thing George Washington did after he took the oath of office was to stoop over and kiss the Bible on which his hand had just rested?

Even in our churches, how many children in Sunday school and church know anything about the two thousand years of Christian history? Where are the missionary stories? What's happened to the heroes and martyrs and stalwarts of the past, whose courage brought the gospel down the ranks to us? How many children grow up learning the Twenty-Third Psalm and the Lord's Prayer? And what has happened to our classic hymns? Our spiritual heritage is slipping away.

Our Theology Is Being Weakened

We must also guard our theology. It's easy for churches to become malnourished in times of spiritual famine. George Barna and his researchers issued a 2020 report warning, "American Christians are undergoing a 'post-Christian Reformation.'" Barna said, "The irony of the reshaping of the spiritual landscape in America is that it represents a post-Christian Reformation driven by people seeking to retain a Christian identity.... The most startling realization . . . is how many people from evangelical churches are adopting unbiblical beliefs."

The report went on to warn, "Evangelicals have traditionally emphasized the importance of seeing the Bible as the infallible, inerrant Word of God. Now, however, 52 percent do not believe in objective moral truth."[1] The researchers concluded, "What used to be basic, universally-known truths about Christianity are now unknown mysteries to a large and growing share of Americans—especially young adults."[2]

For centuries, God's Word has been at the center of Christian preaching. Today, questioning scriptural authority is in vogue, even in certain faith communities. Popular speakers advocate processing God's Word through cultural filters rather than the other way around. Remember, we don't stand in judgment of the Bible. It stands in judgment of us. When we turn our backs on God and His Word, God may turn His back on us. The book of Romans speaks of God giving people over to their sinful wills (Romans 1:18–32). Many in our society will suffer from unintended consequences because of their desire to distance themselves from God's Word.

Our Bibles Are Being Overlooked

According to Dr. Jeremiah Johnston, the average American household owns between three and ten Bibles, but forty-two percent of American Christians are too busy to read them. "As Christians we need to understand the reality of biblical illiteracy, first in our own lives and families but also in the church."[3] In each region of the world, there is a unique challenge to biblical literacy. China shuts down Bible apps and book sales; Islamic nations persecute Bible-reading citizens; and Western hotels are restricting access to the Gideons, who place Bibles in hotels around the world.

That's spiritual famine! People who disregard the Bible may someday get what they want—a society where the Bible is no longer read or proclaimed and where they can freely sin without Scripture confronting their conscience. But they may get more than they bargained for. A society without the moral compass of Scripture will self-destruct from moral decay and decadence.

Our Appetite Is Being Ruined

The reason we're facing a spiritual famine is because our appetite for God's truth is being ruined. In these Last Days, it seems as if Satan has unleashed an invisible spiritual virus that robs people of their appetite for God's Word. But it's worse than that, because it's not just a loss of appetite. It's a total distaste for the Bible. People grab a handful of Scripture, take a bite, find it distasteful, and spew it out like a child spitting out carrots. As likely as not, they'll dub it "hate speech" and attack anyone who offers a bite to others.

God may respond to our lack of spiritual appetite with silence. He doesn't force His words in our ears, and He may withdraw for a time if we lose our appreciation for the privilege of His voice. God's silence may be hardly noticeable at first. You may still remember a time when God spoke to you, but you gradually became aware that you hadn't heard His voice for a long time. If you realize you are in a drought, immediately seek God. Ask Him about needed adjustments in your life so you can once again enjoy fellowship with Him.

By grace, we can stay healthy even during a large-scale spiritual famine. Paul told us to be "nourished in the words of faith and of . . . good doctrine" (1 Timothy 4:6). The psalmist described Scripture as sweeter than honey (Psalm 19:10). And the prophet Jeremiah said, "Your words were found, and I ate them, and Your word was to me the joy and rejoicing of my heart" (Jeremiah 15:16). The Lord gave us a Book containing everything we really need for life and eternity. It makes us wise unto salvation through faith in Christ. It's portable; we can carry it anywhere. It's simple; perfect for children. It's deep; engaging the lifetimes of earth's greatest scholars. And it's yours! Jesus said, "People do not live by bread alone, but by every word that comes from the mouth of God" (Matthew 4:4, NLT).

Where Do We Go From Here?

What, then, should we do when our land is spiritually famished? Near the end of the Bible, the apostle Peter wrote two letters to the churches of his day, penning the final one shortly before his gruesome death by up-side-down crucifixion. As he wrote those last words, one thing was on his mind: making sure no one forgot the message of the gospel or the teachings of Scripture. He said: "I will not be negligent to remind you always of these things, though you know and are established in the present truth" (2 Peter 1:12). Also, Peter wrote, "I will be careful to ensure that you always have a reminder of these things after my decease" (2 Peter 1:15).

Lastly on this topic, Peter said: "I now write to you this second epistle (in both of which I stir up your pure minds by way of reminder), that you may be mindful of the words which were spoken before by the holy prophets, and of the commandment of us, the apostles of the Lord and Savior, knowing this first: that scoffers will come in the last days" (2 Peter 3:1–3).

Peter was leaving the world, but he wanted his message to remain, to never be forgotten, and to be passed down through the generations until Jesus returns. He longed for the gospel to expand, to explode throughout the earth. He wanted to repel spiritual famine. That same zeal must seize us. It must consume the Church of today as we face the world of tomorrow. It must become not so much what we do as followers of Jesus, but who we are. Based on Peter's words, let me give you four "Be's" to put into practice during times of spiritual famine.

Be Burdened

Peter spoke as a deeply burdened man who wanted to make sure his audience was devouring the Word and sharing it with others. He was ready to make every effort as long as he lived. The apostle Peter also gave us another example of what it's like to be burdened for a society facing spiritual famine. He described Lot, who lived in Sodom, as "a righteous man, who was distressed by the depraved conduct of the lawless (for that righteous man, living among them day after day, was tormented in his righteous soul by the lawless deeds he saw and heard)" (2 Peter 2:7–8, NIV).

In a similar way, the apostle Paul walked around Athens and "was provoked within him when he saw that the city was given over to idols" (Acts 17:16). Jesus felt the same burden for His city, crying out, "Jerusalem, Jerusalem, the one who kills the prophets and stones those who are sent to her! How often I wanted to gather your children together, as a hen gathers her chicks under her wings, but you were not willing!" (Matthew 23:37)

We can't do much to alleviate the spiritual famine around us until we have a similar concern within us. We don't to want live in perpetual sorrow, but how we need the compelling love of Christ burning like a fire in our heart for a famished globe. We need a fresh vision for the world. We need to be the Good Samaritan in someone's life.

Be Students

Second, Peter insists we become personal students of Scripture and devour its truth. He said, "As newborn babes, desire the pure milk of the word, that you may grow thereby, if indeed you have tasted that the Lord is gracious" (1 Peter 2:2–3). Peter wanted us to know the nature of

Scripture, which did not originate with human beings, "but holy men of God spoke as they were moved by the Holy Spirit" (2 Peter 1:21).

He told us to search it "intently and with the greatest care," the way the prophets of old studied the Scriptures, earnestly looking for all they could find there about the Lord (1 Peter 1:10, NIV). This means submitting to Scripture as the very foundation of our lives. Peter also told us how studying God's Word would affect us. By pouring over "exceedingly great and precious promises," we will "be partakers of the divine nature, having escaped the corruption that is in the world through lust" (2 Peter 1:4).

Someone said that the best way to teach children to eat well is for them to see their parents thoroughly enjoying a healthy meal. How can we expect the world to develop an appetite for Scripture when we ourselves never become diligent students of the Bible? Bible teacher Warren Wiersbe said, "In all of my conference ministry, I've tried to get people excited about the Bible. There's so much there that people ignore and they shouldn't do that. I find that when I trace the cross references, when I take time to pray and meditate, God says something to me. Then I can share that with others. So the joy of the Bible is not in learning something abstract. The joy of Bible study is seeing your life changed."[4]

Begin today! Learn to read the Bible systematically, study it diligently, apply it correctly, and share it boldly. Jesus said, "Blessed are those who hunger and thirst for righteousness, for they shall be filled" (Matthew 5:6).

Be Shepherds

Peter had a special word of instruction for pastors and Bible teachers: "Shepherd the flock of God which is among you, serving as overseers, not by compulsion but willingly" (1 Peter 5:2). In using the term *shepherd*, he was undoubtedly thinking of his own experience years before when Jesus walked with him along the shoreline of Galilee. The Lord asked him three times, "Do you love Me?" "Yes, yes, and yes!" replied Peter. Jesus said to him, "Feed My sheep" (John 21:15–17).

Let's remember the Bible teachers of Ezra's day: "So they read distinctly from the book, in the Law of God; and they gave the sense, and helped them to understand the reading" (Nehemiah 8:8). Following that pattern would do much to alleviate today's spiritual famine. Christian parents must diligently feed the lambs entrusted to them with the Word of God.

While there are many family devotional resources available, nothing is richer than the frequent habit of sharing with your children what you've found yourself in His Word. The Bible tells us to share the Scripture with our children when we get up and when we go to bed, when we sit at home and when we travel down the road. We're even told to write it on placards and to post it on the walls of our homes (Deuteronomy 6:6–9).

This devil-sent spiritual famine cannot exist among those in whom the Bible's little verses are lived out in real time in front of their children. Peter says, "I will always remind you of these things, even though you know them and are firmly established in the truth you now have. I think it is right to refresh your memory as long as I live" (2 Peter 1:12–13, NIV).

Be Evangelistic

Finally, to ease the spiritual famine in the world today, we have to aggressively give out the Bread of Life. Peter reminds us we have been "born again, not of corruptible seed but incorruptible, through the word of God which lives and abides forever. . . . Now this is the word which by the gospel was preached to you" (1 Peter 1:23–25).

Peter explains his strategy for winning the lost like this: "Sanctify the Lord God in your hearts, and always be ready to give a defense to everyone who asks you a reason for the hope that is in you" (1 Peter 3:15). The way to banish spiritual famine in the world is one person at a time. We turn the tide as we share the gospel of Christ with boldness, ready to give an answer to anyone who asks for a reason for the hope within us. God has warned us of the coming days of spiritual famine, but He has given us living bread to share with the world.

In John 6:27–35, Jesus said: " 'Do not labor for the food which perishes, but for the food which endures to everlasting life. . . . My Father gives you the true bread from heaven. For the bread of God is He who comes down from heaven and gives life to the world.' Then they said to Him, 'Lord, give us this bread always.' And Jesus said to them, 'I am the bread of life. He who comes to Me shall never hunger, and he who believes in Me shall never thirst.' " May God whet our appetite for this bread, and may He use us as relief workers in these days of spiritual drought and inward hunger!

APPLICATION

Personal Questions

1. Read John 6:27–35.

   a. What can you learn from the disciples' response in verse 28?

   b. How does this look lived out in your life, and what can you do to make sure you are diligent in your pursuit of God's will for your life?

   c. What does verse 35 say is the ultimate answer to alleviate the disciples' hunger?

   d. Why is this passage important to a lesson on spiritual famine?

   e. After reading this passage, how can you avoid the spiritual famine plaguing so many people and have spiritual depth in your faith?

2. Read 1 Peter 3:13–17.

   a. What encouragement does Peter give us in verse 14 as we seek spiritual depth in our relationship with God?

   b. What is Peter's strategy for winning the lost in verse 15 that is referenced in the "Be Evangelistic" section?

   c. How can you be prepared to defend the faith as Peter says?

   d. With what attitude are you supposed to do this (verses 15–16)?

   e. What is one part of this that you have struggled with, and how can you be proactive in being faithful to God in this regard?

Group Questions

1. Read Nehemiah 8:7–8.

   a. What is the biblical model for Scripture reading that Nehemiah implements in this passage?

b. How should our churches operate in light of this? Are they succeeding as a whole today in teaching God's Word faithfully as it was done in Nehemiah's day? Discuss.

c. How can our pastors and lay leaders do a better job of teaching the Bible like this? Give examples.

d. Read verse 9. How did the people respond to Scripture?

e. What can we do to have the reverence for Scripture that the Israelites had in this passage?

2. Read 2 Peter 1.

a. What does verse 4 say will happen when we study the Scriptures intently?

b. Verse 4 ends by saying that through Christ we escape the "corruption that is in the world through lust." How can we share that message in a fallen world this week?

c. Read verses 5–9 once again. What do these verses say about depth in our faith? How is it obtained according to this section?

d. What would it look like if everyone around us began to study God's Word with the intensity that Peter tells us to study it?

DID YOU KNOW?

There are ten famine periods in the Old Testament. One of the allures of the Holy Land was its fertile land, but there are numerous times when that fertility suddenly turned into barrenness. Famine was often connected with the Israelites' disobedience, just as spiritual famine comes from the rejection of God's Word. Famine was much fresher on the minds of the Israelites than many of us today because they had lived through and lost family members due to a famine. This made the spiritual famine imagery utilized by Amos, Micah, and even the apostle Paul that much more powerful to them.

Notes
1. Jessica Lea, "Barna: We're Experiencing Another Reformation, and Not in a Good Way," *Church Leaders*, October 8, 2020.
2. "Six Megathemes Emerge from Barna Group Research in 2010," *Barna*, December 13, 2010.
3. Jeremiah Johnston, *Unanswered* (New Kensington, PA: Whitaker House, 2015), 143, 147, 153.
4. Jonathan Peterson, "The Joy of Bible Study Is Seeing Your Life Changed: An Interview With Warren Wiersbe," *BibleGatewayBlog*, March 26, 2019.

LESSON 9

A GEOGRAPHICAL PROPHECY—JERUSALEM

EZEKIEL 5:5

In this lesson we learn about God's plans for the city of Jerusalem and its role in prophecy, and we explore the coming city of New Jerusalem.

The future of Jerusalem is predicted many times in the Bible, yet the current Jerusalem seemingly could be wiped off the map at any moment because of powerful enemies in the region. Jerusalem's importance cannot be overstated, as it is home to Judaism, Christianity, and Islam. Its contested religious significance and the political instability of the region constantly threaten the survival of Jerusalem, but its scriptural significance is unrivaled and its future is glorious.

OUTLINE

I. What Does This Mean?
   A. You'll Be Overjoyed with Its Beauty
   B. You'll Be Overwhelmed with Its Holiness
   C. You'll Be Overcome with Its Savior

II. Where Do We Go From Here?
  A. Stay Fervent in Your Prayer for Israel
  B. Stay Faithful in Your Service and Ministry
  C. Stay Focused on Israel and Jerusalem

OVERVIEW

The prophet Zechariah declared over 2,500 years ago: "Thus says the LORD: 'I will return to Zion, and dwell in the midst of Jerusalem. Jerusalem shall be called the City of Truth'" (Zechariah 8:3). Jerusalem is interwoven like a golden thread into the tapestry of biblical history and future prophecy. Jerusalem is one of the oldest cities on earth, the place where Melchizedek met Abraham, where Abraham offered Isaac, and where Solomon met the queen of Sheba. Countless passages in the Bible detail its prevalence in the revelation of God's will—past, present, and future. Its history lingers in the very air of the city, constantly paying homage to its past while pointing to its future.

By moving the U.S. embassy to this hallowed city, the United States made a historic statement in support of Israel, illustrating a unique union between two of the greatest democracies on earth. Since then, other nations have moved their embassies to Jerusalem, though the decision to do so is controversial. In fact, many politicians and pundits proclaimed the move would lead to renewed conflict in the region. Clearly world leaders understand the importance of Israel, even if they don't believe in the God who has vested Jerusalem with biblical and prophetic significance. Some people wonder why there are such deep emotions about a piece of real estate, yet the city emanates its own unique significance.

Jerusalem is bound up with prophecies from Almighty God. The city of Jerusalem is arguably (and certainly prophetically) the world's most significant city. Jerusalem is mentioned in the Bible 811 times. Its most important names are: the City of David (2 Samuel 5:7, 9), Zion (Psalm 87:2), the City of Righteousness (Isaiah 1:26), the City of the Great King (Psalm 48:2), and the Holy City (Isaiah 48:2; 52:1; Revelation 21:2).

Though Jesus was born in nearby Bethlehem and raised in Nazareth, He visited Jerusalem many times. When our Lord was only a few days old, His parents brought Him to the temple and presented Him to the Lord (Luke 2:21–40). He tarried in Jerusalem at age twelve, spending three nights alone in its darkened streets and conversing by day with the teachers in the temple (Luke 2:41–50). After His baptism, Jesus was taken to Jerusalem by Satan, to the highest point of the temple (Luke 4:9–12).

John recorded four visits of Jesus to Jerusalem (John 2:13–3:21; 5:1–47; 7–10; 12–20), and the other Gospels add important details, particularly regarding the events of the Passion Week. Jesus loved Jerusalem, and He mourned over her unbelief: "O Jerusalem, Jerusalem, the one who kills the prophets and stones those who are sent to her! How often I wanted to gather your children together, as a hen gathers her chicks under her wings, but you were not willing!" (Matthew 23:37) After Jesus's ascension, Church history began in Jerusalem. The book of Acts is replete with references to the activities and sufferings of the early Christians, including Peter and John, in the city of Jerusalem. The gospel spread in concentric circles from Jerusalem, Judea, and Samaria to the outermost parts of the earth (Acts 1:8).

Jerusalem is the center of Israel in the same way our heart is the center of our bodies. No city on earth has captured the world's attention through the centuries like Jerusalem. Ezekiel 5:5 says, "This is Jerusalem; I have set her in the midst of the nations and the countries all around her." Randall Price wrote: "Jerusalem is the city at the center. It is the center of mankind's hopes and God's purposes. God loves it, Satan hates it, Jesus wept over it, the Holy Spirit descended in it, the nations are drawn to it, and Christ will return and reign in it. Indeed the destiny of the world is tied to the future of Jerusalem."[1]

Jerusalem was chosen specifically by God for her role in the history of Israel, in the life of Jesus, and in the events of His return. According to 1 Kings 11:13, Jerusalem is the city which God has chosen. This fulfills the five-fold prediction of Moses in Deuteronomy 12 that God will choose a city as the dwelling place for His great name after the children of Israel possessed their Promised Land (verses 5, 11, 14, 18, 21).

Four other passages uniquely link Jerusalem with Almighty God: (1) "I have chosen Jerusalem, that My name may be there, and I have chosen

David to be over My people Israel" (2 Chronicles 6:6); (2) "For the LORD has chosen Zion; He has desired it for His dwelling place: 'This is My resting place forever; here I will dwell, for I have desired it'" (Psalm 132:13–14); (3) "The LORD loves the gates of Zion more than all the dwellings of Jacob. Glorious things are spoken of you, O city of God" (Psalm 87:2–3); and (4) "Moreover He . . . chose the tribe of Judah, Mount Zion which He loved" (Psalm 78:67–68). There's a biblical sense in which Jerusalem is eternal. It will never die! Jerusalem is God's own unique eternal city.

Jerusalem became the capital of Israel by decree of King David over three thousand years ago. It has remained Israel's capital ever since. Though other nations conquered and settled in the land of Israel, none ever declared Jerusalem their capital. Over the past two thousand years, even during times of occupation and persecution, a Jewish community has resided in Jerusalem and maintained it as their "eternal capital." During the 1948 War of Independence, Jordanian forces conquered and occupied the eastern part of Jerusalem containing the historic Jewish Quarter, the Temple Mount and Western Wall, Hebrew University, and Hadassah Hospital. But in the Six-Day War of 1967, these areas were retaken by Israel, and Jerusalem was reunified. Every prime minister since has declared the city to be "the eternal and undivided capital of the Jewish State."

What Does This Mean?

Jesus will return to Jerusalem at the Mount of Olives, and He will establish His thousand-year reign from Jerusalem. This millennium is referred to as "the kingdom of heaven" (Matthew 3:2; 8:11), "the kingdom of God" (Mark 1:15), "times of refreshing" (Acts 3:19), "times of restoration" (Acts 3:21), "the day of Jesus Christ" (Philippians 1:6), "the fullness of the times" (Ephesians 1:10), and "the world to come" (Hebrews 2:5). Psalm 2 places Jesus in Jerusalem (Zion) during the Millennium. The psalmist writes, "I have set My King on My holy hill of Zion. I will declare the decree: The LORD has said to Me, 'You are My Son, today I have begotten You. Ask of Me, and I will give You the nations for Your inheritance, and the ends of the earth for Your possession'" (Psalm 2:6–8). The prophet Jeremiah added: "At that time Jerusalem shall be called The Throne of the LORD, and all the nations shall be gathered to it, to the name of the LORD, to Jerusalem" (Jeremiah 3:17).

After the Millennium, the ultimate Jerusalem—New Jerusalem—will descend to the new earth to be the capital city of heaven and of our heavenly homeland forever.

John saw "the holy city, New Jerusalem, coming down out of heaven from God" (Revelation 21:2). This is the city anticipated by Abraham (Hebrews 11:16), promised by Christ (John 14:2–3), and awaited by the saints (Hebrews 13:14). This is "the city of the living God, the heavenly Jerusalem" (Hebrews 12:22). Since our resurrected bodies will be physical bodies, as real and tangible as Christ's, they will need a real place and an actual home. Revelation gives us a glimpse of this: "He who overcomes, I will make him a pillar in the temple of My God, and he shall go out no more. I will write on him the name of My God and the name of the city of My God, the New Jerusalem, which comes down out of heaven from My God. And I will write on him My new name" (Revelation 3:12).

Listen as John wrote in awe: "I saw a new heaven and a new earth, for the first heaven and the first earth had passed away. . . . Then I, John, saw the holy city, New Jerusalem, coming down out of heaven from God, prepared as a bride adorned for her husband. And I heard a loud voice from heaven saying, 'Behold, the tabernacle of God is with men, and He will dwell with them, and they shall be His people. God Himself will be with them and be their God. And God will wipe away every tear from their eyes; there shall be no more death, nor sorrow, nor crying. There shall be no more pain, for the former things have passed away.' Then He who sat on the throne said, 'Behold, I make all things new'" (Revelation 21:1–5).

John saw this city already built and descending from above. Jesus referred to this New Jerusalem as "the city of My God" (Revelation 3:12). This city of New Jerusalem is the place Jesus is preparing for us (John 14:1–6). The Bible draws to a close with a breathtaking description of its dimensions, its description, its streets, its vast river, its wondrous throne, its translucent gold, and its glittering light.

You'll Be Overjoyed with Its Beauty

The Bible describes the New Jerusalem as a city built upon a foundation of precious stones. Entry into the city will be through gates of pearl, and the streets will be paved with gold. The light of the city will emanate from the Lamb of God. Near the city center we'll find the tree of life, which has been missing to us since the Garden of Eden. The inhabitants of the city will be able to eat the leaves of the tree, and those leaves will somehow provide a deeper sense of our wellbeing in heaven.

In the very heart of the city, the river of life will pour forth from beneath the throne, flow through the landscape, and delight the whole earth (Revelation 22:1). This is likely the same river mentioned by the psalmist: "There is a river whose streams shall make glad the city of God, the holy place of the tabernacle of the Most High" (Psalm 46:4). The beauty of New Jerusalem will be amplified by its size. The boundaries of the celestial city exceed anything ever envisioned by human engineers. Consider the dimensions of the city itself. It's "a city four-square"—1,500 miles long, 1,500 miles wide, and 1,500 miles high.

You'll Be Overwhelmed with Its Holiness

Three times in Revelation 21 and 22, John calls the New Jerusalem a holy city: (1) "Then I, John, saw *the holy city*, New Jerusalem" (Revelation 21:2, emphasis added); (2) "And he carried me away in the Spirit to a great and high mountain, and showed me the great city, *the holy Jerusalem*, descending out of heaven from God" (Revelation 21:10, emphasis added); and (3) "And if anyone takes away from the words of the book of this prophecy, God shall take away his part from the Book of Life, from *the holy city*" (Revelation 22:19, emphasis added).

John writes: "But there shall by no means enter it anything that defiles, or causes an abomination, or a lie, but only those who are written in the Lamb's Book of Life" (Revelation 21:27). John lists eight kinds of people who will never step foot inside the gates of the New Jerusalem: "But the cowardly, unbelieving, abominable, murderers, sexually immoral, sorcerers, idolaters, and all liars shall have their part in the lake which burns with fire and brimstone, which is the second death" (Revelation 21:8).

The one and only thing that can bar us from heaven is our failure to trust Christ as Savior and Lord. The writer of Hebrews went out of his way to describe the city inhabitants: "You have come to Mount Zion, to the city of the living God, the heavenly Jerusalem. You have come to thousands upon thousands of angels in joyful assembly, to the church of the firstborn, whose names are written in heaven. You have come to God, the Judge of all, to the spirits of the righteous made perfect" (Hebrews 12:22–23, NIV).

You'll Be Overcome with Its Savior

There's so much to anticipate about heaven, but there's one priority above all others—seeing the Lord Jesus Christ. That includes seeing His face, glimpsing His smile, enjoying His fellowship, and worshiping His glory. Revelation 22:4 says, "They shall see His face, and His name shall be on their foreheads." When we die, we can have confidence that we will see the Savior in heaven, in all His glory.

Where Do We Go From Here?

What does all this have to do with us today? How do these prophecies about tomorrow explain the problems we have today? The following sections consist of some lesson-ending calls to action.

Stay Fervent in Your Prayer for Israel

The psalmist wrote, "Pray for the peace of Jerusalem: 'May they prosper who love you. Peace be within your walls, prosperity within your palaces.' For the sake of my brethren and companions, I will now say, 'Peace be within you.' Because of the house of the LORD our God I will seek your good" (Psalm 122:6–9). We must pray for the internal peace of Israel. Only Jesus Christ can bring unity to such a tangle of tongues and tempers, to such a labyrinth of languages, cultures, and passions as is seen in the Old City. We need to pray for the Jews, the Palestinians, the Christians, and all who make this land their home.

Secondly, stay fervent in your prayers for the international safety of Israel and Jerusalem. Modern Israel has been forced to maintain a continual state of warfare throughout its years. Israel has been the single most discriminated against state at the United Nations. Put a map of Israel in your Bible, and remember to pray for its place among the nations.

Stay Faithful in Your Service and Ministry

Christianity and Judaism both encourage us to anticipate the Messiah's coming by concentrating on being godly people and doing acts of kindness. As Peter instructed in the Bible, "Since everything will be destroyed in this way, what kind of people ought you to be? You ought to live holy and godly lives as you look forward to the day of God and speed its coming" (2 Peter 3:11–12, NIV). In a similar way, Isaiah wrote: "Is it not to share your bread with the hungry, and that you bring to your house the poor who are cast out; when you see the naked, that you cover him, and not hide yourself from your own flesh?" (Isaiah 58:7)

Jerusalem is far away for many who will study this lesson. In some cases, it's literally on the other side of the world. Yet as we've seen, all who trust in Christ as their Savior will enter the New Jerusalem. Even now, we're moving toward that wondrous city. It's our eternal destiny. It's our home! For these reasons and more, let's live right now as citizens of New Jerusalem.

Stay Focused on Israel and Jerusalem

As we witness the United States embassy being moved to Jerusalem and marvel at the Abraham Accords—the new alliances Israel has created with the United Arab Emirates, Bahrain, and Sudan—we're witnessing a major shift in the geopolitical landscape of the Middle East. Until recently, the Middle East has been "everybody against Israel." Israel was public enemy number one in the eyes of her neighbors. But it's become obvious that the greatest threat to existence in the Middle East is now the aggressive radical Islamic terrorist nation of Iran. Recent reports thrill us with the numbers of Iranians coming to Christ. But the nation's leadership remains insanely aggressive. The other Arab nations could never survive a conflict with Iran, so, remarkably, they are looking to Israel. So, we must keep our eyes on the chessboard of the Middle East. It's our responsibility to become experts on the land God has marked as the flashpoint of prophecy.

APPLICATION

Personal Questions

1.   Read Revelation 22:6–11.

     a. What blessing does John record in verse 7?

b. How should that influence you as you read this lesson and study the coming End Times prophesied about in Revelation?

c. What is John's response to the fullness of God's revelation coming from the angel (verse 8)?

d. What is the angel's response to his worship in the following verse?

e. What does the angel say about sealing the words of the prophecy he has just revealed to John (verse 10)? In what way is this important to us as Christians?

2. Read Revelation 22:18–21.

a. What do these verses say about those who would add or remove from God's revelation to John?

b. What does this say about the importance of this book of Scripture?

c. How does this change your attitude as you seek to learn from it and navigate through the complex passages?

d. What words of Jesus are recorded in verse 20?

e. How does John follow this statement, and how should you be inspired by this as you also look forward to the return of Christ?

Group Questions

1. Read 2 Peter 3:10–13 together.

a. What does Peter say will happen in verse 10?

b. What are some ways this contrasts with what many people teach about the Last Days on earth?

c. What is Peter's question to Christians like us in light of this prophetic vision of the future (verses 11–12)?

d. What encouragement does he give as a follow-up to this question (verse 13)?

e. Discuss how we can take advantage of this encouragement as we further our walk with the Lord.

2. Read 2 Peter 3:14–18 as a group.

a. What is Peter's answer to the question he asked in verses 11–12 (verse 14)?

b. What warning does Peter give us as we go about our preparation for the Day of the Lord? What solution does Peter give in the following verse for staying strong in our faith and avoiding this potential pitfall (verses 17–18)?

c. What specific ways can we live like this passage commands us to live this week, and how can we encourage each other as we try to live as Peter commands?

DID YOU KNOW?

Jerusalem contains evidence of settlements in the area dating as far back as 4500 BC. One group of Egyptian texts, written over 3,800 years ago, referenced Jerusalem even before it was referenced in the Bible. It has been the scene of over one hundred battles in history, demonstrating its significance in past generations as much as is on display with the present conflicts plaguing Israel. Even to this day, there are ordinances for any new buildings to be covered in Jerusalem stone to maintain the historical appearance of the city. Clearly this city values and appreciates its history as well as its future significance.

Note
1. Randall Price, *Jerusalem in Prophecy* (Eugene, OR: Harvest House, 1991), 74.

LESSON 10

THE FINAL PROPHECY— THE TRIUMPH OF THE GOSPEL

REVELATION 17:14

In this lesson we learn about the glorious triumph of the gospel: Jesus overcoming this world and His followers taking the message to the lost and finishing strong.

The demonic forces currently at work will continue to increase in power until the return of our Lord. But we can take heart in His power and be confident in His ultimate triumph over Satan. He has triumphed over the grave in His death and resurrection, and He will expel the forces of evil forever when He returns. The gospel is spreading all over the earth, and the light of Christ is shining through our lives.

OUTLINE

I. **What Does This Mean?**
   A. The Message of the Gospel Is Transforming
   B. The Work of the Gospel Is Expanding
   C. The Followers of the Gospel Are Maturing

D. The Author of the Gospel Is Preeminent
E. The Theme of the Gospel Is Energizing

II. Where Do We Go From Here?
A. Preach the Gospel with Your Lips
B. Picture the Gospel with Your Life
C. Ponder the Gospel with Your Mind
D. Practice the Gospel with Your Love
E. Finish Strong

OVERVIEW

Billy Graham's ministry covered a turbulent half-century, but he confronted every issue with one thing: the gospel of Jesus Christ. His sermons echo Paul's words: "I determined not to know anything among you except Jesus Christ and Him crucified" (1 Corinthians 2:2).

How can we do the same? The gospel alone can triumph over the many challenges we face. In the early days of the Church, the Jewish high officials in Jerusalem couldn't figure out what to do with the apostles. Israel's most respected rabbi, Gamaliel, told the officials, "Leave these men alone! Let them go! For if their purpose or activity is of human origin, it will fail. But if it is from God, you will not be able to stop these men; you will only find yourselves fighting against God" (Acts 5:38–39, NIV). He spoke true wisdom, and his words have rung true for two thousand years. They are true for us. Our influence, our work, and our service for the Master cannot be stopped.

The Bible says, "Now thanks be to God who always leads us in *triumph* in Christ, and through us diffuses the fragrance of His knowledge in every place" (2 Corinthians 2:14, emphasis added). What a powerful word that is, *triumph*. According to the book of Revelation, this is the ultimate consummation of biblical prophecy: "See, the Lion of the tribe of Judah, the Root of David, has *triumphed*" (Revelation 5:5, NIV, emphasis added).

What Does This Mean?

The focus of this lesson is found in Colossians. After receiving a report about false teachers and weakened doctrine in Colossae, the apostle Paul responded with four glorious chapters about the transcendence of Christ and the triumph of the gospel.

Paul wasn't just writing to Colossae but also to us as he exhorted us never to allow ourselves to be "moved away from the hope of the gospel" (Colossians 1:23). He went on to warn: "Beware lest anyone cheat you through philosophy and empty deceit, according to the tradition of men, according to the basic principles of the world, and not according to Christ. For in Him dwells all the fullness of the Godhead bodily; and you are complete in Him, who is the head of all principality and power" (2:8-10). The principalities and powers are fallen supernatural beings—rulers of the darkness in this age, spiritual hosts of wickedness in the heavenly places (Ephesians 6:12-13). But Jesus Christ is victorious. On the cross and through His resurrection, He "disarmed principalities and powers, He made a public spectacle of them, *triumphing* over them in it" (Colossians 2:15, emphasis added).

He broke the power of him who holds the power of death—that is, the devil—and freed those who were held in slavery by their fear of death (Hebrews 2:14-15). In the Last Days the Antichrist and his cohorts will "wage war against the Lamb, but the Lamb will *triumph* over them because he is Lord of lords and King of kings" (Revelation 17:14, NIV, emphasis added).

Biblical prophecy leads us past chaos and cataclysm to Christ Himself. In Colossians, Paul put it like this: "He has delivered us from the power of darkness and conveyed us into the kingdom of the Son of His love, in whom we have redemption through His blood, the forgiveness of sins" (Colossians 1:13-14). Without Christ, we're in Satan's grip. But when we believe and receive His Good News, He instantly conveys us into His family and into His kingdom.

The Message of the Gospel Is Transforming

This message is life altering. It instantly changed the lives of a handful of people in the town of Colossae, snatching them from the power of darkness and conveying them into the kingdom of light. Two thousand years later, the same gospel is transforming hearts today.

We cannot imagine how many people are saved by the blood of Christ every single day in this world. Only heaven knows that statistic, but each life is radically transformed. Paul told the Colossians, "We heard of your faith in Christ Jesus and of your love for all the saints; because of the hope which is laid up for you in heaven, of which you heard before in the word of the truth of the gospel, which has come to you" (Colossians 1:4–6).

The Work of the Gospel Is Expanding

Furthermore, the work of the gospel is expanding. Paul went on to say, "[The gospel] has come to you, as it has also in all the world, and is bringing forth fruit" (1:6). Even in Paul's day, he saw the gospel spreading and expanding like concentric circles throughout the entire known world. Jesus said, "And this gospel of the kingdom will be preached in all the world as a witness to all the nations, and then the end will come" (Matthew 24:14).

The gospel is yielding unprecedented fruit around the globe. Yes, we've talked about apostasy and the perceived decline of Christianity in the West. But the triumphant gospel is penetrating new areas, and truly amazing things are happening. For example, one report said the Gospel is spreading through Iran at a "sizzling pace." Another report said the Holy Spirit is "on fire" in Iran.[1]

As followers of Christ, we read the news differently than other people. When we hear reports of the Iranian nuclear deal or the ayatollah's apocalyptic threats, we have to remember the Lord is at work behind the headlines, and the gospel is spreading into every corner of earth with its message of triumph.

The Followers of the Gospel Are Maturing

Furthermore, the followers of the gospel are maturing. The apostle Paul told the Colossians he was praying "that you may be filled with the knowledge of His will in all wisdom and spiritual understanding; that you may walk worthy of the Lord, fully pleasing Him, being fruitful in every good work" (Colossians 1:9–10). He asked God to strengthen them with all might and to give them power, patience, and endurance.

How we need that, and how God is doing that! While the world is worsening, the Lord's servants are increasing and His churches are advancing. We have a young generation whose growth in zeal and godliness will be tested but which will triumph in the years ahead.

Jesus said, "I will build My church, and the gates of Hades shall not prevail against it" (Matthew 16:18). Despite all the anguish and abuse of our age, the gospel will triumph through the Church as we mature in Christ and bear fruit in every good work. Never underestimate the power of your local church, for Jesus died to plant it in this world. He rose again to empower it to reach every new generation with His glorious gospel.

The Author of the Gospel Is Preeminent
The Author of the gospel—our Lord Jesus Christ—"is the image of the invisible God, the firstborn over all creation. For by Him all things were created.... And He is before all things, and in Him all things consist. And He is the head of the body, the church, who is the beginning, the firstborn from the dead, that in all things He may have the preeminence" (Colossians 1:15–18).

As we see Jesus more clearly, His gospel gets bigger in our hearts. His death becomes more wonderful. His resurrection becomes more astonishing. Sin becomes more disgusting, and the devil seems more evil. The restoring work of the Spirit gets mightier. The global extent of the gospel becomes more important. The connections between everything within the Bible become clearer. Our yearning for eternity becomes greater. And the love of God becomes more delightful.

Is Jesus truly preeminent in your life? Is He number one? In this careening culture and in these perilous days, we must say as never before: "All to Jesus I surrender, all to Him I freely give." As someone said long ago, "Only in the Christian life does surrender bring victory."

The Theme of the Gospel Is Energizing
Another triumphal note in Colossians sounds like the blast of a trumpet: "Christ in you, the hope of glory" (Colossians 1:27). When Charles Spurgeon preached from this verse, he used a very simple outline.

- The essence of the gospel is: Christ
- The sweetness of the gospel is: Christ in you
- The outlook of the gospel is: Christ in you, the hope of glory

Taken together, this is the triumph of the gospel, and you can make it your own: "Christ in me, the hope of glory!" The moment we proclaim Christ as our Savior, He comes, through His Spirit, to live and reign within us. One day we'll share His glory and have a part in His inheritance, reigning with Him over the new heavens and the new earth.

This hope is the theme of the Gospel, and it's just as certain as the death of Christ. Just as sure as His resurrection. Just as exciting as His return. And just as real as His indwelling Spirit. The New Living Translation says, "And this is the secret: Christ lives in you. This gives you assurance of sharing his glory" (Colossians 1:27).

Where Do We Go From Here?

Whenever we quote the Word of God, we know there is limitless power in every syllable. Because every word of the Bible is inspired, we cling to every verse. So let's highlight five phrases, directly from the book of Colossians, that will tell us where to go from here. Because Jesus is preeminent and His gospel is triumphant, we can live and labor in victory in several critical areas.

Preach the Gospel with Your Lips

As followers of Jesus, we must keep preaching Christ and holding up the cross. Colossians 1:28 says: "*Him we preach*" (emphasis added). We must keep doing that till the end. Verses 28 and 29 read, "[Christ] is the one we proclaim, admonishing and teaching everyone with all wisdom, so that we may present everyone fully mature in Christ. To this end I strenuously contend with all the energy Christ so powerfully works in me" (NIV). This is our calling as Christians, and this is how we respond to the trials of this current world.

To the very end of life, to the very end of time, and to the very ends of the earth, let's use all our strength to preach Him and His triumphant gospel. The Lord has blessed us with the opportunity of reaching what may be one of the last generations prior to His return.

Picture the Gospel with Your Life

We must do the important personal work every day of growing and maturing in Christ, learning from Him, being built up in Him, and abounding with thanksgiving.

Charles Spurgeon called this adorning the gospel. He said, "What is appropriate to the gospel? Well, *holiness* suits the gospel. Adorn [the gospel] with a holy life. . . . The gospel is also to be adorned with *mercifulness*. It is all mercy, it is all love, there is no love like it: 'God so loved the world.' Well, then, adorn the gospel with the suitable jewels of mercifulness and kindness. . . . The gospel also is the gospel of *happiness*; it is called, 'the glorious gospel of the blessed God.' A more correct translation would be, 'the happy God.' Well, then, adorn the gospel by being happy. . . . Adorn the gospel, next, by your *unselfishness*. . . . If you would adorn the gospel, you must love others, love them intensely, and make it one object of your lives to make other people happy, for so you will then be acting according to the spirit and genius of the gospel."[2]

All that is summed up in Colossians 2:6: "As you therefore have received Christ as Lord, so walk in Him." In Colossians 2:6, the word "walk" indicates an ongoing process. Our actions are to consistently align with our words and beliefs. We preach the gospel with our lips, and we picture the gospel with our lives.

Ponder the Gospel with Your Mind

The gospel of Jesus Christ informs not only our actions but also our thoughts. Colossians 3 begins with some of the most positive words ever written: "Since you have been raised to new life with Christ, set your sights on the realities of heaven, where Christ sits in the place of honor at God's right hand. Think about the things of heaven, not the things of earth" (verses 1–2, NLT).

Think of our Lord's present glory, seated at the right hand of God. John saw this image of Him and wrote: "He had in His right hand seven stars, out of His mouth went a sharp two-edged sword, and His countenance was like the sun shining in its strength. And when I saw Him, I fell at His feet as dead. But He laid His right hand on me, saying to me, 'Do not be afraid; I am the First and the Last. I am He who lives, and was dead, and behold, I am alive forevermore. Amen'" (Revelation 1:16–18).

We must set our hearts on this, constantly meditating on the dazzling glory of our triumphant Christ. Meditate frequently on the throne of Christ, and you'll sleep better by night and feel more enthusiasm by day. Set your heart on things above, where Christ is, seated at the right hand of God.

Practice the Gospel with Your Love

God commands this of us in Colossians 3:14–15: "Above all, clothe your-selves with love, which binds us all together in perfect harmony. And let the peace that comes from Christ rule in your hearts. For as members of one body you are called to live in peace" (NLT). Christ's gospel isn't something we simply believe—it's something we do by choosing to love others.

Jesus said, "A new commandment I give to you, that you love one another; as I have loved you, that you also love one another. By this all will know that you are My disciples, if you have love for one another" (John 13:34–35).

Francis A. Schaeffer says about this passage: "Jesus is giving a right to the world. . . . To judge whether you and I are born-again Christians on the basis of our observable love toward all Christians. . . . If people say, 'You don't love other Christians,' we must go home, get down on our knees, and ask God whether or not they are right. And if they are, then they have a right to have said what they said."[3]

We have a triumphant gospel, but those who share it must be clothed in love and carry in their hearts a genuine burden for their neighbors and for their enemies to overcome the venom of sin in the world.

Finish Strong

Colossians ends with a short verse: "Take heed to the ministry which you have received in the Lord, that you may fulfill it" (Colossians 4:17). Let's all put our own name in Colossians 4:17 and fulfill our work. Our Lord's first recorded words as a youngster were, "I must be about My Father's busi-ness" (Luke 2:49). And at the end of His natural life, He said, "I have glo-rified You on the earth. I have finished the work which You have given Me to do" (John 17:4).

We have to complete the work God has assigned us. The apostle Paul said, "My life is worth nothing to me unless I use it for finishing the work assigned me by the Lord Jesus—the work of telling others the Good News about the wonderful grace of God" (Acts 20:24, NLT).

Jesus Christ's triumph trumps all the headlines of history. Despite the title of this study guide, we are not worried about where we go from here. We know Him who has prepared the way and we are more than conquerors through our Lord Jesus Christ. That's the triumph of the gospel.

We're soldiers in the battle now, but one day the Lamb will triumph because He is Lord of lords and King of kings, and He will bring His called, chosen, and faithful followers with Him. As the Tribulation draws near its climax, Revelation says: "They will wage war against the Lamb, but the Lamb will *triumph* over them because he is Lord of lords and King of kings—and with him will be his called, chosen and faithful followers" (Revelation 17:14, NIV, emphasis added).

Oh, may we all be there!

APPLICATION

Personal Questions

1. Read the story of Gamaliel in Acts 5:34–39.

   a. How did Gamaliel approach the issue of the growth of the Early Church?

   b. How do the examples he gives in verses 36 and 37 of failed revolts contrast with the story of Jesus? What does this say about Jesus' power working in the Early Church through His Spirit?

   c. Do you think Gamaliel was convinced that the disciples would leave and their story would fall apart? Or do you think he caught a glimpse of the power of Christ in the testimony of the disciples?

2. Read Colossians 1:9–18.

a. What godly qualities does Paul pray the Colossians will receive?

b. How are those necessary for their ministry to be effective?

c. What does Paul ask the Lord to reveal to the Colossians in verse 9?

d. What does he say this will lead to in their walk with Christ (verse 10)?

e. How does verse 13 describe the dramatic change between our lives before Christ and our lives in Christ?

f. What does Paul say about Christ in verses 15–18?

g. What encouragement can you draw from this passage, and how does it strengthen you in your work in the Lord?

Group Questions

1. Read Colossians 2:8–15 together.

   a. What does Paul repeat numerous times about the power of Christ in relation to our lives?

   b. Discuss why it is still so hard to live a life that is pleasing to Christ after reading such a powerful passage.

   c. What does Paul warn us about in verse 8?

   d. In what ways can this be seen in the world and even the Church around us?

e. What does verse 10 say about our lives in Christ? How does Paul say Christ has triumphed over the world?

f. What does living in triumph look like for us as individuals in the Church?

g. How does verse 11 explain our purification in Christ? How does this differ from the physical way in which many believers thought they were supposed to be redeemed and put into right standing with God?

h. What can we do this week to better live out our new lives in Christ that have "put off" the rule of the flesh?

i. What process did Jesus go through to forgive our sins (verses 13–14)?

2. How can the power of this image challenge us as we seek to live our lives for the Lord?

DID YOU KNOW?

Billy Graham spoke to more than 215 million people in 185 countries. He preached for almost sixty years and was listed on Gallup's most admired people poll sixty-one times (the second-most listed was Ronald Reagan at thirty-one). He received knighthood from Queen Elizabeth II and also received a star in Hollywood. He's spoken to twelve U.S. Presidents, which is more than one quarter of them. However, through all of this fame he was able to stay focused on his most important calling: sharing the Word of God with the masses and imploring them to come to faith in Christ.

Notes

1. Leah Nablo Yecla, "Gospel Making Inroad in Iran Despite Strong Persecution," *Christianity Daily*, November 16, 2020.
2. Charles Spurgeon, "Adorning the Gospel," *The Spurgeon Center*, May 26, 1887.
3. Francis A. Schaeffer, *The Mark of the Christian* (Downers Grove, IL: InterVarsity Press, 2006), 23.

Leader's Guide

Thank you for your commitment to lead a group through *Where Do We Go From Here?* Being a leader has its own rewards. You may discover that your walk with the Lord deepens through this experience. Throughout the study guide, your group will explore new topics and review study questions that encourage thought-provoking group discussion.

The lessons in this study guide are suitable for Sunday school classes, small-group studies, elective Bible studies, or home Bible study groups. Each lesson is structured to provoke thought and help you grow in your knowledge and understanding of God. There are multiple components in this section that can help you structure your lessons and discussion time, so make sure you read and consider each one.

Before You Begin

Before you begin each meeting, make sure you and your group are well-versed with the content of the lesson. Group members should have their own study guide so they can follow along and write in the study guide if need be. You may wish to assign the study guide lesson as homework prior to the meeting of the group and then use the meeting time to discuss the lesson.

To ensure that everyone has a chance to participate in the discussion, the ideal size for a group is around eight to ten people. If there are more than ten people, try to break up the bigger group into smaller subgroups. Make sure the members are committed to participating each week, as this will help create stability and help you better prepare the structure of the meeting.

At the beginning of the study each week, start the session with a question to challenge group members to think about the issues you will be discussing. The members can answer briefly, but the goal is to have an idea in their mind as you go over the lesson. This allows the group members to become engaged and ready to interact with the group.

After reviewing the lesson, try to initiate a free-flowing discussion. Invite group members to bring questions and insights they may have discovered to the next meeting, especially if they were unsure of the meaning of some parts of the lesson. Be prepared to discuss how biblical truth applies to the world we live in today.

Weekly Preparation

As the group leader, here are a few things you can do to prepare for each meeting:

- *Make sure you are thoroughly familiar with the material in the lesson.* Make sure you understand the content of the lesson so you know how to structure group time and are prepared to lead group discussion.

- *Decide, ahead of time, which questions you want to discuss.* Depending on how much time you have each week, you may not be able to reflect on every question. Select specific questions that you feel will evoke the best discussion.

- *Take prayer requests.* At the end of your discussion, take prayer requests from your group members and pray for each other.

Structuring the Discussion Time

As the group leader, it is up to you to keep track of the time and keep things moving along according to your schedule. If your group is having a good discussion, don't feel the need to stop and move on to the next question. Remember, the purpose is to pull together ideas and share unique insights on the lesson. Make time each week to discuss how to apply these truths to living for Christ today.

The purpose of discussion is for everyone to participate, but don't be concerned if certain group members are more quiet—they may be internally reflecting on the questions and need time to process their ideas before they can share them.

If you need help in organizing your time when planning your group Bible study, the following schedules, for sixty minutes and ninety minutes, can give you a structure for the lesson:

Section	60 Minutes	90 Minutes
WELCOME: Members arrive and get settled	5 minutes	10 minutes
GETTING STARTED QUESTION: Prepares the group for interacting with one another	10 minutes	10 minutes
MESSAGE: Review the lesson	15 minutes	25 minutes
DISCUSSION: Discuss group study questions	25 minutes	35 minutes
PRAYER AND APPLICATION : Final application for the week and prayer before dismissal	5 minutes	10 minutes

Group Dynamics

Leading a group study can be a rewarding experience for you and your group members—but that doesn't mean there won't be challenges. Certain members may feel uncomfortable discussing topics that they consider very personal and might be afraid of being called on. Some members might have disagreements on specific issues. To help prevent these scenarios, consider the following ground rules:

- If someone has a question that may seem off topic, suggest that it is discussed at another time, or ask the group if they are okay with addressing that topic.

- If someone asks a question you don't know the answer to, confess that you don't know and move on. If you feel comfortable, invite other group members to give their opinions or share their comments based on personal experience.

- If you feel like a couple of people are talking much more than others, direct questions to people who may not have shared yet.

You could even ask the more dominating members to help draw out the quiet ones.

- When there is a disagreement, encourage the group members to process the matter in love. Invite members from opposing sides to evaluate their opinions and consider the ideas of the other members. Lead the group through Scripture that addresses the topic, and look for common ground.

When issues arise, encourage your group to think of Scripture: "Love one another" (John 13:34); "If it is possible, as far as it depends on you, live at peace with everyone" (Romans 12:18, NIV); and "Be quick to listen, slow to speak and slow to become angry" (James 1:19, NIV).

About
Dr. David Jeremiah
and Turning Point

Dr. David Jeremiah is the founder of Turning Point, a ministry committed to providing Christians with sound Bible teaching relevant to today's changing times through radio and television broadcasts, audio series, books, and live events. Dr. Jeremiah's common-sense teaching on topics such as family, prayer, worship, angels, and biblical prophecy forms the foundation of Turning Point.

David and his wife, Donna, reside in El Cajon, California, where he serves as the senior pastor of Shadow Mountain Community Church. David and Donna have four children and twelve grandchildren.

In 1982, Dr. Jeremiah brought the same solid teaching to San Diego television that he shares weekly with his congregation. Shortly thereafter, Turning Point expanded its ministry to radio. Dr. Jeremiah's inspiring messages can now be heard worldwide on radio, television, and the Internet.

Because Dr. Jeremiah desires to know his listening audience, he travels nationwide holding ministry rallies and spiritual enrichment conferences that touch the hearts and lives of many people. According to Dr. Jeremiah, "At some point in time, everyone reaches a turning point; and for every person, that moment is unique, an experience to hold onto forever. There's so much changing in today's world that sometimes it's difficult to choose the right path. Turning Point offers people an understanding of God's Word as well as the opportunity to make a difference in their lives."

Dr. Jeremiah has authored numerous books, including *Escape the Coming Night* (Revelation), *The Handwriting on the Wall* (Daniel), *Overcoming Loneliness, Prayer—The Great Adventure, God in You* (Holy Spirit), *When Your World Falls Apart, Slaying the Giants in Your Life, My Heart's Desire, Hope for Today, Captured by Grace, Signs of Life, What in the World Is Going On?, The Coming Economic Armageddon, I Never Thought I'd See the Day!, God Loves You:*

He Always Has—He Always Will, Agents of the Apocalypse, Agents of Babylon, Revealing the Mysteries of Heaven, People Are Asking . . . Is This the End?, A Life Beyond Amazing, Overcomer, Everything You Need, and *Forward.*

stay connected to the teaching of
DR. DAVID JEREMIAH

· · · · · · · ·

Publishing | Radio | Television | Online

FURTHER YOUR STUDY OF THIS BOOK

· · · · · · · · ·

Where Do We Go From Here? Resource Materials

To enhance your study on this important topic, we recommend the correlating audio message album, study guide, and DVD messages from the *Where Do We Go From Here?* series.

Audio Message Album

The material found in this book originated from messages presented by Dr. Jeremiah at Shadow Mountain Community Church where he serves as senior pastor. These ten messages are conveniently packaged in an accessible audio album.

Study Guide

This 144-page study guide correlates with the messages from the *Where Do We Go From Here?* series by Dr. Jeremiah. Each lesson provides an outline, an overview, and group and personal application questions for each topic.

DVD Message Presentations

Watch Dr. Jeremiah deliver the *Where Do We Go From Here?* original messages in this special DVD collection.

To order these products, call us at 1-800-947-1993
or visit us online at www.DavidJeremiah.org.

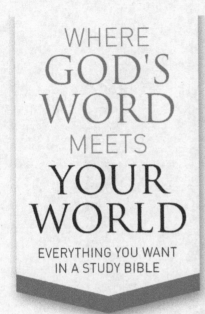
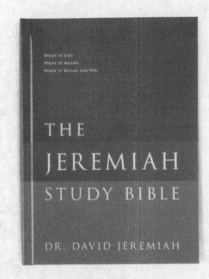

COMPANION BOOK TO ENRICH YOUR STUDY EXPERIENCE

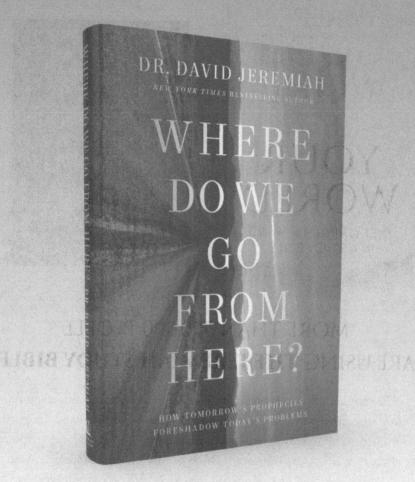

ISBN 9780785224198

Available wherever books are sold

W Publishing Group

New Bible Study Series from Dr. David Jeremiah

The Jeremiah Bible Study Series captures Dr. David Jeremiah's forty-plus years of commitment to teaching the whole Word of God. Each volume contains twelve lessons for individuals and groups to explore what the Bible says, what it meant to the people at the time it was written, and what it means to us today. Out of his lifelong ministry of *delivering the unchanging Word of God to an ever-changing world*, Dr. Jeremiah has written this Bible-strong study series focused not on causes, current events, or politics, but on the solid truth of Scripture.

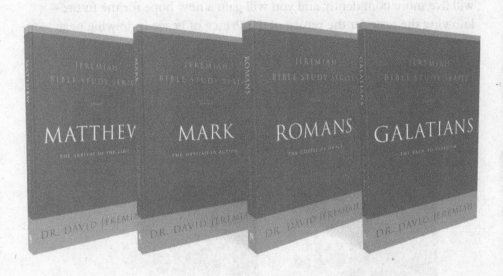

Available now at your favorite bookstore.

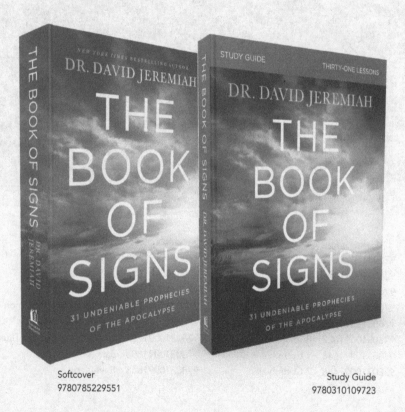

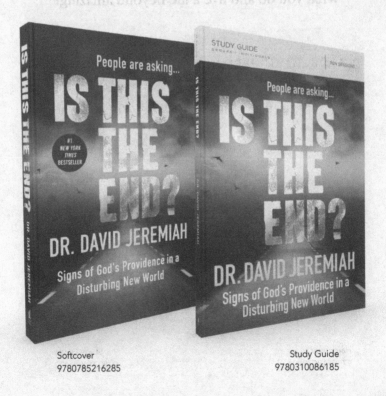

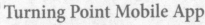